What Became of Little Jackie Smith?

A True Story Continued

D0706996

By Vickie Smith Odabashian

Contents

Prologue

On Friday, June 29, 2001, I called my dad from my cell phone. I was excited to tell him I had just been to the top of the Security Bank Building and was even allowed to stand outside on the ledge. I described the experience of over-looking the street from sixteen stories above – the sun felt warm, there was a slight breeze, and I could hear the faint sound from the traffic below, but overall, it was a quiet place.

Earlier that morning, after a last-minute walk through a park delayed my intended departure time by about an hour, I left Southern California for a six-hour drive to my home in Northern California. Three hours into my trip, I decided to stop at the half-way point, the city of Fresno, for food and a bathroom break. I exited Highway 99 to a street I hoped would take me into downtown Fresno; I turned onto a one-way street and entered the first parking garage I saw. After parking, I walked out of the garage, and to my surprise, I was standing directly across the street from the Security Bank Building. The doors to the main entrance were propped open; I didn't hesitate to take that as an invitation.

Once inside the building, I met the owner and told her I had recently written and published the life story of my grandmother, Victoria, who jumped to her death from the top of the Security Bank Building (also known as the Pacific Southwest Building) in 1950. I didn't live in Fresno and had only seen the building from the outside; I was hoping to see the interior. It just so happened, the owner of the building was

Security Bank Building, Fresno, Calif.

preparing to show two local television news reporters the renovations being done to the building, so she invited me to join them as they looked around.

I had dressed that morning for summer travel; I wore baggy shorts, flip-flops, and a T-shirt, my hair was in a sloppy ponytail, and I wasn't wearing make-up. I felt like a ragamuffin compared to everyone else, who were dressed in business causal, but I knew the opportunity would not likely present itself again, so I accepted the owner's offer. I chose to hang toward the back of the group so I wouldn't be near the television camera crew when they captured footage of the building.

The owner of the Security Bank Building explained to the reporters who I was and why I was there, and together everyone went up the elevator to the fifteenth floor. We walked up a staircase to the sixteenth floor and followed the owner to a little room with a small door that opened to the outside and onto the ledge wrapping around the building top. Stepping out into the sunlight, sixteen stories off the ground, I was beside myself with excitement. I had read the newspaper accounts of my grandmother's last moments, had even written about them in my book, and though the owner was speaking at the time, I couldn't stop myself from blurting, "I'm sorry for interrupting, but we just took the same route as my grandmother." The owner stopped talking, so I continued, "She went up the elevator, ascended that staircase, left her coat in that little room, and came out here through this window." I pointed over the barrier. "She climbed over there where she sat and prayed before she jumped."

Everyone looked at me with their chins dropped until one of the television reporters interrupted the silence by telling me he wanted to interview me. I looked down at my clothes, put my hand to my ponytail, and thought, *Oh man!* I asked,

"Now?"

My reluctance was obvious, so we arranged to meet at a future date. The reporter for the other news station scheduled an interview with me as well, and the owner offered to allow us back to the top of the Security Bank Building for the interviews.

Most fathers would have been uneasy knowing his child just stood on the top of the tallest building located between Los Angeles and San Francisco, but not my dad. In fact, he was thrilled, even knowing my three daughters (his only grandchildren), thirteen-year old Courtney, ten-year old Moriah, and six-year old Jordan, had accompanied me. That's because in the mid-1990s, my dad began to play a dual role in my life – he was my dad, and he also became my teammate, as we delved into the past and searched for information about his mother's life and tragic death. Though I did most of the legwork, my dad contributed ideas, offered guidance, helped collect resources, and gave me confidence; that is why my dad reacted to the news of my girls and me standing atop the same building from which his mother leapt to her death fifty-one years before with, "That's neat, Sweetheart."

A week later, with makeup applied, hair styled, and proper attire, I was able to tell television reporters the story of how a family secret was uncovered while I was investigating my grandmother's suicide, and how I wrote a book about it. I was interviewed and filmed at the base of the Security Bank Building, on the staircase leading to the top floor, on the ledge at the top of the building, and several miles away at my grandmother's gravesite by Monte Francis from the NBC affiliate, KSEE, and Keith Garvin from the ABC affiliate, KFSN.

Appearing on the news in Fresno with my grandmother as the subject matter was important to me for several reasons. First, I knew there were people in Fresno who learned of my grandmother's death through the extensive news coverage or heard about it through word of mouth, and some who had even witnessed her suicide leap. I also knew that the reported cause of my grandmother's suicide left a lot of unanswered questions. I wrote the answers to some of those questions in my book, and my appearance on Fresno news stations let people know how they could find those answers if they wanted to. Secondly, I knew that my grandmother's father and sisters, the informants to the coroner and the media immediately following my grandmother's death, and the source of the word-of-mouth spread over many years, intentionally gave limited and one-sided details in hopes of hiding a family secret. Some of those informants still lived in Fresno, and my appearance on their local television news station let them know that the destructive lies they hid were exposed and written about in a book honoring my grandmother's memory, and was a heads up, of sorts, that maybe they should figure out how they're going to explain themselves. Lastly, I figured the exposure on television wouldn't hurt book sales.

The events in summer 2001 were the beginning stages of my book tour, and over the next two years, I was asked to present my grandmother's biography at bookstores, church-es, cultural organizations, and political events throughout

California and eastward into Michigan, Washington D.C., New York, Massachusetts, and Rhode Island. In my travels, I discovered that people found my grandmother's story intriguing, as I had hoped when I wrote about her, because the book raised questions about my grandmother's life and death, and in the end, also answered many of them. However, the more I traveled, and the more people I spoke with, additional questions arose about my grandmother's life story — questions I didn't have immediate or simple answers to.

They were questions about my dad.

My dad was a ten-year old boy, referred to at the time as Jackie, and sometimes as Little Jackie, who had been taken by his father to an undisclosed location in the months prior to his mother's death. Jackie's disappearance was a noted cause for my grandmother's despair, so his name was mentioned alongside hers in the media coverage of her very public suicide. As I wrote in my grandmother's biography, many people openly expressed concern about Jackie's whereabouts, and at least one person searched for him shortly after his mother died but to no avail. Another person later said that for forty-eight years she had wondered whatever became of Little Jackie Smith. Other people, however – those who were hiding the family secret – sat quietly and let it be. In their minds, Jackie's disappearance while in the care of his father was just as well.

Because my book focused mostly on my grandmother's life and death, a child's disappearance was the last thing readers knew about Little Jackie, so when given the opportunity to ask me questions, many expressed their curiosity about my dad's life after his mother died. The most common questions asked were, "What was your dad's life like after his mother's suicide?" and "What did your dad make of his life?"

I understood their interest because I, too, occasionally heard about or read stories in which children were involved or were victims of a tragic experience, one that likely turned their lives upside down; years later, I would sometimes wonder whatever happened to those children, and what impact did that type of childhood trauma have on the rest of their lives. The difference with my dad's story, however, was that I *was* the one who knew some of what my dad's life was like after his childhood trauma, and for the information I didn't have, I was the mostly likely person to have access to the answers.

While still traveling for speaking engagements with my grandmother's biography, I posed the "What became of Little Jackie Smith?" question to my dad. He was more than happy to answer, or at least begin the answer, because our discussion was followed by numerous additional meetings with lots of storytelling and interviews in which a journey from child-hood tragedy through a life of public service was revealed, as were genuine demonstrations of faith, unconditional love, and dedication to remembrance. It wasn't long before I noticed similarities between my dad's life story and some of the adventures experienced by the fictional character, Forrest Gump. My dad's life story was also one in which the most beloved qualities of another fictional character, Andy Taylor of Mayberry, were real; qualities that were welcomed and cherished by a family, a community, and people around the world.

My dad had so much to say during the times we spent together, I realized that to adequately answer the questions about his life after my grandmother's death, a sequel would need to be written. I doubted it would be too difficult for me to do. Afterall, I wrote my grandmother's biography over a two-year period, and because I'd never met her, a lot of that time was spent conducting genealogical and historical research. My dad, on the other hand, was the primary source of information for his life story, and I had unlimited access to him, so I figured I could get my dad's biography completed in the same amount of time as my grandmother's.

I was wrong! Writing about my dad, someone I knew well and shared a life with, was much harder, and over time one of the biggest obstacles I faced was my own interference. As a daddy's girl, being objective about my dad's life was difficult. Even subtly, when not obviously biased in his favor, I often added my own praises for his achievements, and I criticized those involved in his setbacks. I also had a difficult time accepting that *his* story was not our story, and whenever I wrote in first person, I projected my own perspective or recollection into my dad's life experience. I wasted so much time with this issue, eventually, I had no other choice but to kick myself out of first-person storytelling, and, instead, I wrote his biography in third person.

Little Jackie Smith Became...

CHAPTER 1
A Team Player

In autumn 1951, Jackie Smith turned twelve-years old. His mother, Victoria, passed away a year and a half earlier, and after that time, he lived in a home with his father, then the homes of his father's two sisters, foster homes, and back with his father again. Shortly after his 12th birthday, Jack entered the seventh grade, and he decided he no longer wanted to be referred to as Jackie or Little Jackie, the nicknames he was given as a child, but rather wanted to be called Jack, his legal birth name.

Jack began the school year living in an apartment with his dad, Smitty, and his 24-year-old stepmother, Jean, near Golden Gate Park in San Francisco. Smitty was working on the construction of the Russian Hill Tunnel, and Jean worked part-time jobs to supplement the income. A few months into his seventh-grade school year, Jack's family moved to a different part of the city where his new school gave him a view of Alcatraz from his classroom. Jack found the view intriguing because, at the time, Alcatraz was a working federal prison famous for having housed some of the country's most notorious criminals, such as Al Capone and Machine Gun Kelly.

A short time later, Smitty and Jean separated. Jack was able to remain in his school, but he and Smitty had to find a more affordable place to live. Their new home became a motel in an area known as the Tenderloin District where there were a lot of bars, night clubs, strip clubs, and high rates of crime. The entrance to their motel was located next to the main door to Original Joe's Restaurant and Bar on Taylor Street — a family owned establishment which, despite its location within a mix of lower-class citizens, appealed to people of middle and upper social classes. The room Jack shared with his dad was located on the second floor of the building where the bright, neon lights of the Original Joe's restaurant sign were just outside the window where Jack slept.

A few months into life at the motel on Taylor Street, Smitty accepted a job for work on a power plant hydro-tunnel in Palmer, Alaska. Jack didn't want to change schools again, so the motel managers and the other long-term motel guests made Smitty an offer – if Smitty paid for Jack's room at the motel, prepaid food at a local diner, and provided a plane ticket to Palmer, Alaska, in early June, they would take care of Jack until the school year was over. Each of them would take on certain responsibilities: the landlords would make sure Jack's room was comfortable; a man named Penny would wake up Jack for school each day; another man would accompany Jack whenever he went fishing; and the middle-aged lady would make sure Jack's laundry was done.

Jack thought it was a good idea, but at first, Smitty did not. Eventually, however, Smitty was persuaded to give it a try — but not without first laying down a threat. Penny was a homosexual, and he would be sharing a bathroom with Jack. This gave Penny's guests easy access to Jack's room. Smitty told Penny he didn't want any of his friend's molesting his son. Smitty, a forty-year old, broad-shouldered, six-foot-tall construction worker, was not ordinarily violent, but he told Penny he would come back and kill him if anything happened to his son. Penny and the others agreed to keep Jack safe.

When asked about it later, Jack said, "I had all my assorted friends—my surrogate parents, if you will—of different persuasions. They were social outcasts, but the neatest people you'd ever want to meet. The landlord and landlady were alcoholics but very considerate. I shared a bathroom with Penny, the homosexual, and my other buddy was a Filipino drug addict. I was his fishing buddy. My fourth surrogate was a middle-aged lady. She was a prostitute."

Jack's caretakers were considered social outcasts, and as a nearly orphaned child, Jack knew he was looked upon as one, too. But that didn't matter to Jack; as a team, they all worked well together. And Jack learned a valuable lesson – even if we have little or nothing to our names, there is always someone who can benefit from what we do have. With that belief in mind, Jack decided to help those who had less than he did, so after school and on weekends, Jack rescued injured pigeons; he kept a cage on top of the motel building where he housed and treated the injured pigeons until they were well enough to be set free.

Jack was also there for his caretakers whenever they needed help in return. For example, sometimes the prostitute lady felt she needed to protect herself in her line of business. Jack later said, "When she wanted to impress a gentleman, she would ask me if I would pretend to be her son. She said she was meeting this man, but she wanted me to be there with her as her son, and after a few minutes of her talking to this man, I would ask if I could go to so-and-so's house. If the answer was 'Yes,' that meant the meeting was going well, and I could leave. If she told me 'No', that meant the meeting was not going well. Both times, I was told 'Yes, you can leave now.'"

Though the prostitute may have occasionally pretended to be Jack's mother, he never forgot who his real mother was. In fact, Jack had one important object to remember her by — a gold signet ring with his initials, JLS, on it that Victoria wore; she gave it to Jack before she was arrested and taken to the mental facility several months before her death. The ring fit pre-teen-Jack's finger, so he wore it every day.

Jack found reminders of his mother in other ways as well. Fresno, his former hometown located in the central valley of California, consisting of a population of about 50,000 people spread out among a large span of agricultural landscape, was a lot different than San Francisco's skyscrapers and a population closer to a million people. However, when Jack wandered a mile or so out of the Tenderloin District and into the upper-class shopping area of Union Square looking for injured pigeons, he saw women who carried themselves much like his mother had. Victoria was a woman of modest means, but she always dressed nicely, styled her hair, and made herself presentable whenever she went out in public.

In the San Francisco Tenderloin District itself, there were other reminders of Victoria. As Jack walked the streets in his neighborhood, all genres of music came from the countless nightclubs — one of the most famous of which was Black Hawk, a jazz club in which big-named artists like Thelonious

Monk and the Gerry Mulligan Quartet later recorded music, and it was located only three blocks from Jack's motel room. Whenever Jack walked past that or any of the other night clubs and heard the song *Blue Moon* being played inside, he was instantly taken back to times with his mom. Throughout Jack's childhood in the 1940s, Victoria loved to take him to the theater where, prior to the film starting and during intermission, a live band would play music. She always requested they play her favorite song, "Blue Moon." As Victoria sang the words to Jack, he felt a deep sense of love and adoration from her.

The music for the song *Blue Moon* was originally written for two movies in the early 1930s — with changing lyrics to match the movie scenes. The lyrics were rewritten and titled *Blue Moon* for singer Connee Bosworth who released it as a single in 1935 when Victoria was twenty years old. Four years later, the year Jack was born, Harpo Marx played *Blue Moon* on a harp in the movie *At The Circus*. Mel Torme changed it a bit by adding a male vocal to *Blue Moon* in a 1948 film — then recorded and released it in 1949. Later that year, just a few months before Victoria's suicide, *Blue Moon* was featured in the movie *East Side West Side*.

Though the experience may have been frightening for some, for the remainder of the seventh grade, Jack was comfortable living alone in his motel room. He got up for school each day, he fished with his buddy whenever he wanted, his laundry was kept clean, and he felt safe. Jack later said, as though he had simply been living at a poor man's boarding school, "Those were my protectors, and I was loving life. For a young kid, they were the neatest people. And when the school year ended, they did just as they had promised. They put me on a plane for Alaska."

Jack started his eighth-grade school year living with Smitty in Palmer, Alaska, a town of about 800 people located in a remote U.S. territory (Alaska had not yet become a state). Palmer was a sharp contrast to the city of San Francisco, but after the neon lights, vehicle traffic, and variety of social classes that came with life in a big city, Jack enjoyed the simplicity of a town with no paved roads and a jail located beneath a small theater. Jack described turning thirteen-years old in Palmer where there was "…one bar and it would close down on Tuesday nights for our teen club meetings. I think our Boy Scouts meeting was held there too. The father of one of my friends was the U.S. Marshall."

During the school year, Smitty and Jack returned to Northern California. Jack was placed in a foster home and a new school because Smitty couldn't take a child to the mining camp he worked in. A short time later, Jack moved to Santa Barbara where Smitty was living with his new girlfriend and her children. Still in the eighth grade, Jack was enrolled into Santa Barbara Junior High School. When Smitty and his girlfriend broke up, Jack and his dad moved back to Northern California and settled in Sacramento. In a city of about 150,000 people, Smitty worked as a taxicab driver for a privately-owned company until he was fired for transporting booze to a whorehouse—which, according to Jack, wasn't an uncommon side job at the time. Smitty's firing led Jack and Smitty into homelessness, so they lived on the banks of the

Sacramento River where Jack described food as being in such short supply that, "...any food, even a potato, was a welcomed sight." Smitty was approached on more than one occasion by people suggesting he place Jack back in foster care, what Jack described as being "dumped," but for some reason, that time, Smitty chose not to.

Smitty started working as a cab driver again—but this time for Yellow Taxi, a competitor to his former employer. When he had no money, the other homeless had shared what food they had, so when Smitty earned his first paycheck, he bought bread for all the people in their homeless encampment. Smitty's second paycheck earned him enough money to pay for tickets to the all-night movie theater, so that's where he and Jack slept each night. With the following paycheck, Smitty bought a car, so he and Jack slept in it. After that, Smitty made enough money to rent an apartment in downtown Sacramento. Throughout it all, Jack made sure he got up and went to school each day, and he completed his eighth-grade school year.

In the summer of 1953, Smitty accepted a job out of state, so Jack was placed in a foster home again, this time on a dairy farm twenty-five miles northeast of Sacramento. A short time after Jack arrived, his new foster parents asked him to care for the dairy farm while they went on vacation. It was a lot of work for a thirteen-year-old boy to do by himself, but Jack was out of school for the summer, and he didn't mind helping. When the foster parents returned from vacation, Jack thought he would finish out the summer doing a few chores on the dairy farm and hanging out with his friend, Ed, who lived nearby, but the foster parents had other plans in mind. They told Jack he owed them money for his room and board, and they expected him to continue taking care of their dairy farm for them.

Up to this point, Jack's foster home experience was a relatively good one. In 1941, when Jack was a toddler, Smitty had abandoned his family so Victoria was a working, single mother. Her income was not enough for her to provide for her son on her own, so she was forced to place him in the care of foster services during the week. Victoria rented a small apartment and made sure to take the bus to visit her son every weekend. Sometimes they spent time together at his foster home; other times Victoria took Jack with her for the weekend. They went to her apartment in downtown Fresno and played and roller-skated in nearby parks, they went swimming at the community pool, had lunch at a diner, snacks at an ice cream shop, movies at the theater, and occasionally Victoria took Jack to family functions at her parents' home or the homes of her sisters and their families so Jack could play with his cousins.

As an infant, Jack's first foster parents were an older couple who had several teenage and young adult children of their own. Jack felt loved in their home. A few years later, Jack was placed in a foster home with a woman known as Mrs. Black. Unlike Jack's first foster home where he was the only foster child, at Mrs. Black's, he was one of several foster children of different ages and races. When asked about it later, Jack said he liked the diversity at Mrs. Black's home, what he referred to as "a mixed bag."

When Jack entered kindergarten, he saw his mom on week-ends but knew nothing about his father's whereabouts. The year was 1944, and, except for a few children whose fathers were away fighting in World War II, Jack was in a different situation than most other children in his kindergarten class. Still, Jack didn't feel deprived. He looked at life simply — he had a stable home, he felt loved by the adults around him, and he got to play with other kids. That was mostly all he wanted at the time. When asked about it later, Jack said, "You're living away from your mom, but you see her all the time. Other people become part of your family. It seems normal."

As a teenager, when faced with the dilemma at the dairy farm-foster home, Jack did not agree with what his foster parents were trying to make him do; he thought it was just plain wrong. Jack didn't believe his new foster parents wanted to help a foster child, but rather, wanted an "un-hired hand" to do their work. Jack figured if he was going to have to work and go to school, he was going to do it on his own terms and not theirs, so he ran away. Jack made his way back to downtown Sacramento and knocked on the apartment door of one of Smitty's ex-girlfriends. At this point, the woman had a new boyfriend and a baby, but she offered to let Jack to sleep on her couch if he was willing to babysit when she needed him. Jack accepted her offer. He also got a job washing dishes at a restaurant owned by Smitty's friend, Bill.

Jack turned fourteen years old in August of that year, and the following month, he enrolled himself into the ninth grade. Jack went to school each day, and he worked two jobs. In his spare time, Jack rode his bicycle 25 miles into the foothills on

Highway 40 to visit his friend, Ed, who lived near the dairy farm from which he had run away. Ed's parents were often gone on weekend getaways so Jack, Ed, and some of Ed's siblings spent those weekends partying, which is where Jack first started smoking cigarettes and had his first few bouts of excessive drinking.

At the time, Smitty was working at a mining camp in the town of Bishop (near the California/Nevada border) when he decided to call and check on his son at the foster home. That's when he found out Jack had run away six months earlier. Smitty made some phone calls to his friends in Sacramento and located his son. Smitty said to Jack, "I can't let you do this. You can't live by yourself."

Jack's friend, Ed, asked his parents if Jack could live with them. Ed's parents had their own children at home at the time, and another teenage boy, a friend of Ed's, was living with them, but they agreed to take in Jack, too, so Jack was transferred to Placer Union High School.

One night, while Jack was living at Ed's house, Ed's other friend, the teenage boy who was living there before Jack moved in, tried to date one of Ed's sisters. This upset Ed's parents, so they told the boy he had to leave. Ed was angry at his parents for kicking his friend out, so Ed said, "If he's leaving then I'm leaving too!" Ed then volunteered Jack to join them in rebellion. He said, "Come on, Jack, let's go!"

Jack didn't really want to leave, but he said, "Well, my dad is working in Bishop. Maybe we can get a job there."

The next morning, Ed, Jack and the other teenage boy waited in the bushes until the school bus passed. Then, with a suitcase filled with canned goods, they began hitchhiking. A man pulled over and told the boys he could take them as far as Reno but he was tired and needed to sleep. Ed was a licensed driver, so he got into the driver's seat, the man moved to the passenger's seat, and Jack and the other boy rode in the back.

The man slept until they arrived in Reno, then the boys got out of his car and started hitchhiking again. They got a ride to Carson City, and they were sitting on the side of the road eating a can of beans for dinner when a Carson City Police Officer pulled up to them. The boys told the officer they were going work in Bishop. The officer, a large-built Native American man, suspected there was probably more to their story than they were telling, so he took them to the police station to call their parents. Jack gave Smitty's phone number to the officer. During that conversation, the officer seemed to get confused. He asked Smitty, "Is your son running away from home or to home, sir?"

That evening, all the boys were transported by bus back to Ed's house where Ed's parents called them idiots. The following night, the boys went to the local pool hall to brag about their excursion, and they were all back in their classes on the next school day.

In the summer of 1955, five years after Victoria's suicide, Smitty moved to Oroville, a small town with a population of just over 5000, located in Northern California, 60 miles north of Sacramento. Smitty was working on the construction of the Oroville Dam and had remarried again. Smitty and his new wife, June, lived in a home on Grand Avenue, so Jack moved in with them, and at the beginning of his junior year, just after turning sixteen-years old, he enrolled into Oroville High School.

To get to school each day, Jack rode his bike down Grand Avenue, over the bridge that crossed the Feather River, and up the hill to the high school. He came home to cooked meals from a kind stepmother, and Jack was finally beginning to experience life as a normal teenager. Unfortunately, however, that was short-lived. Smitty and June separated in the spring of 1956 and informed Jack that they would both be moving out of Oroville. Jack told Smitty he did not want to go back into a foster home, he didn't want to leave Oroville, and he didn't want to change schools again. Jack wanted to live on his own, and this time, Smitty agreed to let him do it.

Jack rented a cabin near the railroad tracks about a mile from Oroville High School, and he worked at nearby Currier Bros Market to pay his rent. It was a simple man's home—limited furniture and no extra dishes or utensils beyond what Jack needed for himself. But it was his. Jack no longer had to conform to the rules of another, and he didn't feel like an intruder in someone else's home. He was determined to take care of himself entirely, but he also knew his uncle, George (Smitty's brother), and George's wife, Avis, were not far away. Jack knew Uncle George and Aunt Avis relatively well because they had been neighbors in Sacramento when Jack was ten years-old and his mom was arrested and taken to a mental facility shortly before her death. During Jack's senior year of high school, George and Avis lived on Highway 70, eleven miles south of Oroville in a small mobile home park known as Robinsons Corner, so they were close enough to help if Jack needed it.

Jack went to school each day, played for his high school baseball team, joined the high school band, and the French Club. Outside of school, he bowled, hiked and fished with his friends. Jack was among the minority of teens who smoked cigarettes, but he also fit in with the other teens and the general culture of Oroville. Jack was invited by some of his friends to attend church at The First Christian Church of Oroville, so he did — and he loved it! Jack began attending church regularly with his friends, and a month before his 17th birthday, he was baptized by the church pastor, Don Meyer.

Throughout Jack's senior year of high school, he sang the base voice in the church choir. He enjoyed the evangelism, the comfort of having a church family, and Pastor Don Meyer became a father figure to him. Jack had already developed a heart for service, such as when he rescued injured pigeons in San Francisco's Tenderloin District, and as his high school graduation date approached, Jack set his sights on a future in Christian ministry. Before the end of the school year, Jack completed the application process and was accepted to bible college.

As Jack and his classmates readied for high school graduation, they scheduled photo sessions for their senior portraits. Preparation for the photo shoot reminded Jack of a portrait session he had with his mom when he was young. Victoria was a trained cosmetologist, so even on a normal day, she always made sure Jackie's hair was styled. After picking him up from the foster home for the weekend and riding into

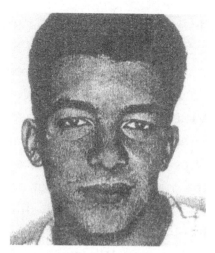

Jack Smith's Oroville High School transcript photo

Little Jackie Smith portrait, circa 1940s (photographer/studio unknown)

JACK SMITH
Activities:
Basketball 1
Wrestling 2
Band 1-3
French Club 4

Oroville High School yearbook, 1957

Victoria Smith portrait, circa 1940s (photographer/studio unknown)

downtown Fresno by bus, she would usually take him into a café and request a glass of water, then take her comb and dip it in the water and start combing back his hair until it was damp and slicked. Outside, on the sidewalk in the sun, Victoria would take out her jar of hair gel and start working it through Jackie's hair. All the while, he would be looking up at people walking by. Those who looked over would grin at the mother preening her child, and with the part just right, hair slicked back and the little wave in front, she would point to his reflection in the window and say, "Now doesn't that look good?" When asked about it later, Jack said, "What's a little kid going to say but 'uh-huh?'"

When Victoria took her son for their portrait session together, she bought him a leather newsboy cap, and she positioned it on his head to make certain his dark wavy hair could be seen at his hairline and few ringlets hung near his ears. Victoria zipped up Jack's matching leather flight jacket just high enough that the shirt beneath it was slightly exposed. During Jack's junior and senior years of high school, he preferred a more casual attire of denim pants and white T-shirt with his pack of cigarettes rolled up in the sleeve. Jack's high school appearance was later described by classmate and baseball teammate, Glen Toney (pictured in the team photo), as being handsome like Hollywood star James Dean. However, Jack knew his mother would not approve of that type of look for his senior portraits, so he treated the moment with the same importance his mom would have if she was there. Jack arrived for the photo session much like his classmates – he wore a suit, tie, and tie tack, and had his

First row, left to right: J. Shipe, J. Pryor, W. Overley, B. Dugger, H. Washington, J. Sawyer. Second row: J. Hayes, K. Williamson, B. Post, T. Nafsiger, S. Huston, J. Thompson. Third row: R. Roberts, G. Toney, J. Owens, D. Bartley, J. Smith, G. Fore. Fourth row: J. Jennings, D. Andoe, H. Bass, K. Williams.

Baseball Team Photo, Oroville High School yearbook, 1957

hair cut short into a more conservative-style crew cut.

The day of Jack's high school graduation, June 7, 1957, the *Oroville Mercury* newspaper announced that Oroville High School graduation ceremonies would begin at 8:30 p.m. in Bechtel Field. The town was preparing for a historic celebration, as it was the first outdoor graduation ceremony in the history of Oroville High School—a monumental event, and the entire community was invited to attend. That day, the newspaper featured a story titled, "Weary, But Happy, The '57 Seniors Look Back As Commencement Day Nears." That certainly applied to Jack; he looked back and felt accomplished. From one day to the next beginning in his early school years, Jack wasn't certain whose house he would be living in (or whose hotel or car for that matter), who would be parenting him, or where his next meal would come from — but one thing he knew was going to happen, he was going to apply himself in school. Despite constantly being uprooted, school was the constant in Jack's life.

Jack knew his mother would be proud on that day because she had instilled in him the importance of an education. Jack knew Smitty would be proud of him, too, because although Smitty didn't pursue an education for himself, he respected all the hard work his son put forth. Jack wished both of his parents could be with him that day, and maybe his mom was somehow watching from Heaven, but as for Smitty, Jack hadn't heard from him since he left Oroville the year before. At least he had his Uncle George and Aunt Avis nearby. They, too, knew that Jack set his sights on a high school diploma at a very young age, and they personally witnessed many of the obstacles Jack overcame to reach his goal, so when they opened the newspaper on the day of Jack's graduation and found photos of all 230 graduating seniors, they were thrilled to scroll through and see that one of them was Jack.

A few hours before Jack's high school graduation ceremony was set to begin, he heard a knock on his cabin door. He opened it to find his dad, Smitty, and his stepmother, June, standing on his porch. Smitty took time off from work at a mining camp in Nevada, and though they were divorced by this time, he and June arranged a time and place to meet, and they traveled from out of town to see Jack graduate. Each expressed their pride in him and presented him with a gift —

a piece of hardcover Samsonite luggage. Jack was touched, especially when he realized they had planned their return to Oroville in advance because, like the ring his mother gave him, the Samsonite had Jack's initials, JLS, embossed on a plate near the handle.

Little Jackie Smith Became...

CHAPTER TWO
A Loving Husband and Father

In the spring of 1965, Jack was twenty-five years old, a single man working in construction. When not at work, he spent his spare time drinking coffee and socializing with friends at the Thrifty Diner. One day, Jack sat in a booth having lunch alone when an attractive young woman entered the diner. She was accompanied by Bill, an acquaintance of Jack's. As the couple passed Jack's table, Bill and Jack greeted each other and started a brief conversation. Bill introduced the young woman as Ann, his coworker at nearby Grant's Department Store. Jack invited them to join him, and they all had lunch together.

Jack and Ann continued to run into each other at Thrifty Diner. Over coffee, lunch or sometimes dinner, a friendship grew, and they began to share personal information about their lives. Jack told Ann that he was raised in Fresno until his mother died when he was ten years old. He explained that his dad, Smitty, and foster parents took care of him after that, and that he moved around a lot. Jack explained that he and his dad moved to Oroville in 1955 and that he graduated from Oroville High School in 1957.

Jack told Ann that after high school, he wanted to continue his education. He knew that his mother's father was highly educated and could speak several languages, and his mother always emphasized the importance of an education. Jack gave his life to Jesus in high school, and he wanted to help people, so he enrolled at San Jose Bible College. Jack told Ann that his father's family was not as interested in higher education; they preferred manual and skilled labor jobs, and Jack shared a story of Smitty's brother, Uncle George, driving him to San Jose for his first semester in bible college. When they passed through an agricultural area, Uncle George pointed to people working the crops and said, "Look at those people out there making money. Don't you want to do that?" Jack replied, "No. I want to go to college."

Jack chose to attend San Jose Bible College because his pastor at the time, Don Meyer, was an alumnus of the college and a board member who recommended the school to graduating teens. So, in the fall of 1957, Jack and several of his friends were among the 122 students enrolled in the college that school year. San Jose Bible College classes began at each weekday at 7:30 A.M. and ended just before lunch at 12:20 P.M. Class schedules included daily chapel at 9:30 A.M. for an hour of singing, praying, fellowship, and preaching. A large part of the culture of San Jose Bible College was music. Choirs, quartets and trios were formed from the student body and sent out for ministry to local churches, camps, youth rallies, and conventions. Some of the groups made recordings of their music. When not in class and singing or preaching in church, Jack drove a truck for Goodwill.

Living near the college campus, Jack was only fifty miles south of San Francisco, so one day he decided to drive to the motel in which he lived on Taylor Street when he was in the seventh grade. He discovered that most of his former caretakers had moved on, but the alcoholic managers and Penny were still there. Jack told them he was training to become a Christian minister, and he thanked them for all they had done for him.

Every day of Jack's week was busy except for Saturdays, so that is when he and his friends squeezed in their fair share of partying. Over time, it was more partying than Jack believed was fitting for someone who was preaching on Sundays, and by the end of the school year, he questioned his plans to work in ministry. Though Jack projected a spirit of love, and that, combined with his welcoming smile, seemed perfect for a prospective minister, he realized ministry wasn't the route for him. When asked about it later, Jack said, "I had too much respect for the position, and it wasn't in me to follow up on it. I bowed out. I wasn't ready to make that commitment. It wasn't there, and I wasn't going to fool them or myself."

Jack left San Jose in the summer of 1958, a time when communism was spreading like a global wildfire, causing already Cold War between the United States and the Soviet Union to grow more intense. Jack was visiting his dad at Smitty's family homes in the towns of Purdy and Nixa, Missouri, when he told Smitty he didn't want to return to college in the fall but instead intended to join the military. Smitty knew there was talk of a possible draft looming, and out of concern that his son would be drafted and not able to choose his preference of the branch of military, he supported Jack's decision to enlist. Smitty said, "And if you're going, it's better to ride than to walk."

So, Smitty took Jack to a recruiter's office in St. Louis, where Jack joined the Navy. Shortly thereafter, Jack packed his Samsonite and headed to bootcamp. He told Ann he was trained to work as an airplane mechanic on the Grumman Tracker, a plane equipped with sonar that operated from aircraft carriers and searched the seas for Soviet submarines. Jack became a crew chief and spent a lot of time flying in and out of a Naval Station in China Lake, Calif., and training aboard the USS Hornet in Long Beach, Calif.

In 1961, shortly after John F. Kennedy became president, suspicion arose around the possibility that the United States was responding to rising escalation of tension in the Far East. First reported in Honolulu, a city nearing the 20th anniversary of the attack on Pearl Harbor and obviously a location especially concerned about war in the Orient, the media mentioned suspicion over the USS Kearsarge leaving port at Pearl Harbor several weeks before planned. Two days later, the "Laos War" was being downplayed by the State Department, but the day after that, March 30th, news outlets in Honolulu reported that men from the 1st Marine Brigade left Hawaii and appeared to be ready to fight.

By the end of April, media outlets made it clear the USS Kearsarge was in the oceans of the Far East among the US Navy's 7th Fleet. A short time later, Jack was transferred from Viking Squadron 41 to Viking Squadron 21, the Fighting Redtails, and was sent on deployment aboard the USS Kearsarge in the South China Sea. There, throughout the summer of '61, while the Marines and Army were on the ground in Laos, Jack and his fellow seamen conducted war training exercises in hopes of discouraging communist leaders from continuing advancement further into Laos. And the tactic worked, at least temporarily, because the countries went back to negotiating.

There were more than 1800 men on the USS Kearsarge, and Jack considered the conditions relatively pleasant. The ship was equipped with a chapel, dining halls, stores for clothing and personal items, a tailor shop, a shoe repair shop (known as the cobbler shop), a library, a fully equipped hospital, and a printing plant. The Kearsarge was like a small city — perfect for someone like Jack who realized he preferred simple living and a small-town feel.

Outside of discussions about trainings and war, a Navy ship like the Kearsarge, with men of all ages and races out on the ocean for several months in the summer of 1961, set the stage for intense music debates. One song released that year took Jack back to memories of his childhood and his mom — the release of The Marcels' doo-wop version of "Blue Moon." Elvis's rendition in the mid-1950s was known for crossing the song into the rock genre, but like the original, it still maintained a slow tempo. The Marcels doo-wop, however, was a rhythm and blues version in which they sped up the tempo and added lyrics that included the rhythmic repeat of words like *bomp, ba, dang, da, do,* and *dip.*

Because The Marcels' version of *Blue Moon* added a completely different feel to the song, some of the older folks preferred covers of the song similar to the jazz-influenced original, like the flawless rendition sung by Ella Fitzgerald in

1956, the instrumental version released on a Glenn Miller medley compilation album in 1958, or Sam Cooke's version released in 1960. But the younger soldiers, like Jack, whose teen years were musically influenced by rock and roll and R&B, loved the changes made to "Blue Moon." And so, too, did the mass of listeners around the United States. The Marcels' version reached number one on several pop and R&B charts. Jack thought his mom would have liked it, too, but would have still preferred the original.

In the Navy, Jack was a self-disciplined, respectful, hard-working, and dedicated sailor who earned a Good Conduct Medal while he was aboard the Kearsarge. He spent his 22nd birthday in Kobe, Japan, while the USS Kearsarge was at port hosting tours of the ship and a luncheon for American and Japanese foreign exchange students. The war exercises and the rest of life at sea went without incident for the people aboard the USS Kearsarge — except near the end of their tour of duty. While en route back to the United States, the USS Kearsarge was refueling the USS Evans, a destroyer escort, when the two ships collided. Damage was minimal, but the USS Kearsarge's return was delayed. Three days after that collision, near San Diego, a helicopter performing a routine flight between the USS Kearsarge and the mainland crashed off the coast of Imperial Beach — all four men on board the helicopter were killed. The following day, anxious family and friends greeted the crew of the USS Kearsarge, as it returned to its home port in Long Beach.

Navy life seemed to fit Jack well, but like Christian ministry, Jack didn't believe military service was his calling either.

Above: Jack Smith, early twenties
Left: Jack Smith, U.S. Navy

So, when his initial four-year commitment came to an end in 1962, at the rank of E-5 — Petty Officer 2nd Class, Jack decided not to re-enlist. While many of Jack's shipmates returned to the Pacific Ocean to retrieve an astronaut, Walter Schirra, from the water after he orbited the earth six times on the Mercury-Atlas 8, Jack returned to Oroville to be close to his family. Once again, Smitty was working on the Oroville Dam construction project and had purchased a Victorian home in downtown Oroville. Smitty's brother, George, still lived south of Oroville with his wife, Avis; Smitty's sister, Gracie, lived in Sacramento with her husband, Wilbur.

Jack moved into Smitty's house on an historic road lined with shade trees that grew so tall they formed a canopy over the street. After working a short time in the lumber industry, Jack joined Smitty in his construction job on the Oroville Dam project. Both understood the importance of a dam to stop the uncontrolled flow of the Feather River. When Jack first moved to Oroville at the beginning of his junior year of high school in 1955, he rode his bicycle over the bridge crossing that river. When winter came, that route to and from school became challenging because storms wreaked havoc on the area, and the river rose to dangerous levels. Flooding occurred periodically in years prior, but 1955 was one of the deadliest winters on record — particularly south and downstream from Oroville.

During their talks at Thrifty Diner, Jack learned that Ann was born and raised on the rural outskirts of Little Rock, Arkansas. She was the oldest of five children and a sophomore in high school when her family moved to Oroville. Ann had picked cotton as a child, and like Jack, she despised working the crops, so she made sure to stay in school; Ann graduated in 1960 when Jack was in the Navy, so they had never crossed paths at Oroville High School. Ann's parents divorced a short time after they moved to California. Her mother married again and had another child, but that marriage failed. Her mother married a third time, and it was their home in which Ann was living. Most of Ann's immediate family lived in Oroville; her father, her mother and stepfather, two aunts and uncles, her sister (who was married with two children) and her two youngest brothers. Two of Ann's other brothers were away in the military — one was fighting in Vietnam.

There were a lot of similarities between Jack and Ann. Like Jack, Ann was friendly and sociable, but also relatively shy. A thin but shapely 5′ 6″ frame, Ann modeled for a short time but didn't pursue it professionally because she was uncomfortable being the center of attention. They also enjoyed the same kind of music, mostly popular music, R&B, and rock and roll. There was, however, one obvious difference between them: Jack had an easy-going, slow to anger manner while Ann had a feisty, spirited side — especially when she got mad. It seemed, however, that their differences balanced each other out.

Eventually, Jack worked up the nerve to ask Ann out on a date. She wanted to date but told him they first needed to have a talk. She told a story of graduating from Oroville High School, marrying a Navy man, and moving with him to San Diego. They divorced less than two years later, so Ann moved to Los Angeles for a couple of years where she was in another relationship. She had only recently returned to Oroville, and although it wasn't obvious yet, Ann was several months pregnant. The man she was seeing in Los Angeles didn't want the baby, so Ann moved back to Oroville to raise the child on her own and be near her family.

Jack wasn't as experienced with relationships as Ann. He dated occasionally in high school and during his year at San Jose Bible College. When asked later about his dating life in the military, he said he dated occasionally but nothing serious. He did find it rather comical, however, to tell a story of certain ladies who were especially nice at the ports the USS Kearsarge stopped at during deployment to the far east. Jack said some of the women in the bars there knew the ships' schedule better than the soldiers. The offers given to him by some of those women were generous, but Jack did not partake. He said, "I was too shy."

The difference between Jack's dating experience and Ann's relationship history reminded him of a story he heard about his own parents. When Victoria and Smitty met, Smitty was twenty-three years-old and had been married and divorced already, at least once; he also had his fair share of other intimate relationships. In fact, when Jack became an adult, Smitty's sister, Gracie, told Jack that his father had been such a womanizer before he met Victoria, he had contracted a venereal disease. Gracie took Smitty to the doctor, and they were told the treatment would make him sterile. Victoria, on the other hand, was twenty years-old and had never been in a serious or intimate relationship, but she didn't hold Smitty's past against him. She fell in love with him, and though he told her he was sterile and would never be able to have children, she married him anyway in 1936. Three years later, she was surprised with a blessing, a son she named Jack.

As an adult, Jack was a handsome man with a beautiful smile. He was a sought-after man, but he never met anyone he was seriously interested in until he met Ann. Jack chuckled at the fact that the woman he wanted to date happened to be pregnant, but just like his mother accepted Smitty despite his extensive experience with relationships, Jack accepted Ann too. So, they started dating. When asked about it later, Jack said, "I wasn't going to not date her *just* because she was pregnant."

As Ann's belly grew, so, too, did her relationship with Jack. When out in public together, people assumed they were married and expecting a child together; neither Jack nor Ann corrected them. For those who knew either of them before they were dating, it may have raised an eyebrow or two, but no one made an issue of it. Jack didn't feel like he needed to explain anything, and though he was a rule-follower in life, he was never afraid to violate social norms if his intentions were good and it was a loving thing to do.

In October 1965, Ann went into labor, and Jack was in the hospital waiting room with Ann's family. After six short hours, it was announced that Ann had given birth to a baby boy; she named him Alan. Ann was living in her own apartment, so after the birth, Jack spent time there helping her care for her newborn. Ann found it amusing that Jack and Alan resembled each other. Jack had black hair, brown eyes, and an olive and brownish skin complexion — Mediterranean features he inherited through his mother's ancestry — and Alan had a head full of dark hair and brown eyes, partly due to his biological father's Mexican heritage. When Jack and Alan were out in public, most people assumed Alan was Jack's biological child. Again, Jack didn't correct them.

Ann and Alan also spent a lot of time with Jack at the Victorian-style home he shared with Smitty. When Alan was a few months old, and Ann and Jack had been dating for about a year, she thought things were very serious between them. But then, Ann was at Smitty's home when she overheard Smitty ask Jack, "You don't want to marry a woman with a child, do you?"

Jack was surprised at Smitty's question; his dad wasn't usually the type of person who was critical of choices other people made, but where his son was concerned, however, Smitty wasn't quite as open-minded. When Ann noticed that Jack remained quiet and didn't answer his dad's question, her feelings were hurt; Ann broke up with Jack, grabbed her son, and she went home. A week later, Smitty and his sister, Gracie, went through Ann's checkout line at Grant's Department Store. Smitty told Ann he missed seeing Alan and asked if she would bring him to his house later that evening. Ann agreed to stop by, though she made sure to tell them she would have to cancel a date to do it. While Ann and Alan were at Smitty's that night, Jack came home from work, so he got to see them too. The following day, Ann answered a knock at her apartment door. It was Jack! He brought with him a marriage proposal, and that day, in March 1966, Jack and Ann drove to Carson City, Nevada, and got married.

A few months into their marriage, Jack took Ann and Alan on vacation to Tijuana, Mexico. On their way, driving through central California, they stopped in Fresno so Jack could visit his mother's grave. By that point, Ann knew more about Jack's childhood and the circumstances that led up to his mother's death. Sixteen years had passed since Jack lost his mother and was cut off from her family. He had always been curious about what became of his mother's siblings and his cousins, and he hoped they had been curious about what became of him, too, so while in Fresno, Jack decided to make contact.

Jack remembered the name of his mother's oldest sister, Grace, so he looked her up in Fresno City phone book. After a short call from a phone booth, Jack and his family were

Jack holding Alan

standing on his Aunt Grace's doorstep with his wife and son. Grace seemed pleased to see Jack again, and he was happy to reconnect with her. They reminisced on times Jack spent with family at her house when he was young, and Jack remembered his grandparents and the names of several of the cousins he played with as a child.

Jack knew very little about the details surrounding his mom's suicide, so little that when completing the family history form for his enlistment in the Navy, he wrote that his mom was deceased, and the cause of death was "unknown." He was a child living in Southern California at the time of his mom's death in Fresno, and he was only told that she jumped from a building top. At that point in his life, in his late twenties, Jack still had no idea his mother's suicide was public, he didn't know his parent's domestic troubles were put on public display in the news, nor did he know his name was part of the story. Jack was secretly hoping Grace might talk about his mom's death, give more insight into his mom's state of mind before she died, and offer some explanation as to why his mom had to place him in a foster home instead of her siblings taking him into their homes, but she didn't mention any of it.

Grace talked about what a good person Victoria was and what a "stinker" she thought Smitty was. Grace also gave Jack pictures from when he was a little boy — mostly of him and his mom. Each picture had their nicknames written on the back, Vickie and Jackie. Also, at Grace's house that day, was Grace's nineteen-year-old daughter, Linda; she was only a toddler at the time of Victoria's death. During Linda's childhood, she heard stories about her aunt's suicide and her long-lost cousin, Jack, so she was intrigued by his visit, so Linda sat quietly during Jack's visit with her mom, but paid close attention to everything being said.

That day, Grace talked to Jack about a family fight that began two years after his mother's suicide. In 1952, Jack's grandfather, George, was old and sick, and in January, he died. Jack's grandmother, Rosa, who was also old and sick, died in July. Jack's aunt, Victoria's youngest sister, Dorothy, died from cancer in November of the same year, shortly after giving birth to her first son, Gus Jr. Grace told Jack how hard the deaths were on the family, and it was worsened by the battle over their inheritance that caused a division among her and some of her siblings.

Before Jack left Fresno that day, he went to the courthouse and looked up records pertaining to his grandparent's estate when they died — which coincided with the months Jack was a twelve-year old living alone in a motel in San Francisco's Tenderloin District. In the documents detailing his grand-parents' estate, Jack read his name and his cousin's name, Gus (the son Dorothy gave birth to shortly before her death), listed among those entitled to a share of George and Rosa's estate. Apparently, Victoria's siblings fought among themselves over the division of their own portions of the in-heritance. Additionally, the amounts specifically allotted for the children of the two deceased daughters, Victoria and Dorothy, were also divided between the adult siblings. Jack already had quest-ions about why his mother's family allowed him to live in foster homes and didn't take him in when he was a child, and the news of them keeping his portion of the inheritance left even more of a bitter taste in his mouth, but he didn't let it ruin his vacation; Jack, his new wife, and their son continued their trip to Tijuana, Mexico.

Six months after Jack and Ann were married, Ann was pregnant again. In May 1967, ten years after Jack's name and

Jack, Ann, and Alan in Tijuana, Mexico, 1966

high school senior portrait appeared in the *Oroville Mercury* Newspaper as a member of the Oroville High School graduating class of 1957, his name appeared in the *Oroville Mercury* Newspaper again. This time it was featured under the boldfaced heading of "statistics" as it was announced, "A daughter born to the wife of Jack Smith."

Though the newspaper did not mention it, the baby was named Vickie in honor of Jack's mother, Victoria. Thirty-years later, when Jack was asked why he decided to name his daughter after Victoria, Jack said of his mother, "I always thought she was a wonderful lady."

Despite Jack's disappointment with his mom's family, he did as promised when he left Grace's house that day — to remain in contact about the child he was expecting. Jack mailed his Aunt Grace a picture of his son, Alan, and his

Alan and Vickie, 1967

newborn baby girl, Vickie. Grace replied that she was happy to hear of the new addition to Jack's family and that naming his daughter in honor of his mother was heartwarming. For no known reason other than lack of continued effort from either person, contact between Jack and Grace ended a short time later.

In the summer of 1967, the Grammy-nominated Motown female recording group The Supremes released a compilation album of songs written by a famous songwriting duo; the album was titled, "The Supremes Sing Rodgers and Hart." For many, the most recognizable tune on the album was the iconic song "Blue Moon." Dean Martin and Frank Sinatra recorded the song a few years earlier retaining the song's ballad roots, but with Diana Ross on lead vocals, The Supremes' big-band sound, seamless harmonies, and classy vocal elegance added a whole new element. The album reached the top of the Billboard pop and R&B albums charts a short time after Vickie's birth.

Little Jackie Smith Became...

CHAPTER THREE
A Servant

Butte County is located on the western slope of the Sierra Nevada Mountain Range in Northern California. The east side of the county is in the mountains and moves west through California's famous golden rolling hills into the flatlands portion of the northern tip of the Sacramento Valley. The Feather River runs from the mountains into the valley. Oroville is the seat of Butte County and was established on the banks of the Feather River at the base of the mountains during the 1850s Gold Rush era — a valley location from which supplies could be taken to goldminers in the mountains. Eventually lumber and agriculture, primarily olives, became the town's economic base.

Because of winter flooding in the valley lands, plans to dam up the Feather River a few miles east of the town of Oroville were under discussion when Jack first moved to Oroville as a junior in high school in fall 1955. A few years later, while Jack was away at college and in the military, construction on the Oroville Dam began. In 1962, when Jack was discharged from the Navy, Smitty was a construction worker on the power-plant portion of the dam. By 1963, Jack was working along-side his dad.

When Jack first moved to Oroville in 1955, sporting events — particularly baseball games — were the center of the excitement in the town. Housing communities were divided by race and social economic status, but sports brought every-body together. The culture of good sportsmanship in Oroville began many years before Jack moved there, signified by the 87 feet long and 33 feet wide, bright white concrete letter "O" placed on a mountainside in the late-1920s. The "O", which hovers over the city of Oroville, was built by Oroville High School alumni, Morrow Steadman, who wrote in his 1929 high school yearbook that he hoped the "O" would remind students of "cooperation and teamwork, both on the athletic fields and in our school activities."

Education was also a high priority to Oroville residents, and because the high school was integrated, it, too, was a place that helped erase racial divides—so much, in fact, prior to Jack moving to Oroville, the older brother of Jack's high school friend, Glen Toney, had been Oroville High School's first Black student body officer—a remarkable accomplish-ment considering, at the time, the early fifties, so many other African Americans across the United States were fighting for integration in the schools and racial equality. Additionally, considering African Americans made up only about 5 percent of Oroville High's student body (and an even smaller percentage of school staff), it was also a testament to the exceptional work of one young man.

From the late 1950s, when Jack left Oroville for bible college in San Jose, through the early-to-mid-1960s, when he returned from service in the military, the population of Oroville increased from 5,000 to 8,000 people, due primarily to an influx of laborers for construction of the Oroville Dam. As a result, people from around the country brought their own

The Feather River traveling west toward the city of Oroville, as seen from the top of the Oroville Dam.

Oroville Dam (white strip of concrete on the right-hand side of the photo) and the Oroville "O" hovering over the city of Oroville on side of Table Mountain (white spot on left-hand side of photo as seen from a field north of Gridley).

personal beliefs and values with them, and the culture of Oroville shifted. Racism existed in Oroville during the 1950s, but after the mass of newcomers, it worsened, and more people in the community frequented bars (saloons and taverns, as they were called), and there was an increase in disputes and violent conflicts. The peace and love movement and the LSD-driven drug culture had not hit Oroville like it had larger cities, such as San Francisco, but mind-altering substances were beginning to trickle into Butte County. Increased numbers of young people who were clean and sober when they left Oroville for college or the military were returning and with a dependence on alcohol, marijuana, and other drugs.

Despite the changes, Jack knew the old values he admired about Oroville were still present, so, it was there where he decided to establish some roots. In 1965, Jack was having coffee and reading the newspaper at Thrifty Diner when he saw a hiring advertisement for the Butte County Sheriff's Department. Thrifty Diner happened to be the place where Butte County deputies and other law enforcement officers spent their down time; it had a large parking area from which officers could easily hop in their cars and race off to an emergency. Jack watched time and time again as law enforcement personnel, some of whom he was conversing with at the time, dropped what they were eating or drinking, ran outside and raced off in their patrol cars with lights flashing and sirens blaring. The idea of that type of adrenaline rush appealed to Jack, but he believed that becoming a person who could keep the peace in a town of growing incidents of chaos was a way he could give back to the community that had treated him so well.

At the time he saw the advertisement, Jack had been hoping to get out of construction work to a more career-oriented job, and though Christian ministry and Navy life didn't suit him, he wanted to go back into public service. Law enforcement sparked his interest, and he hoped to use it as a way of smoothing over the rough patches in the community, so he applied. Jack passed the written exam and the first oral exam. During the second oral exam, he got into an argument with the person interviewing him. Jack later said, "...because I was right, and he was wrong. I think he was trying to piss me off just to see if I would stand by my conviction. And I did. And I got the job. I gave up an $800 per month job for a $400 per month job, but I was thinking long-term."

In October 1965, eight days before Alan's birth, Jack graduated from the Feather River Police Academy, having completed courses in Ethics, Criminal Law, Search and Seizure, Vehicle Codes, Traffic Accident Investigation, Crowd and Panic Control, Beat Patrol and Observation, Field Notetaking, Defensive Tactics, Crime Scene Search and Recording, Arrest Techniques, Firearm Use, Jail Procedures, Interviews and Interrogations, Juvenile Procedures, Report Writing, Basic Police Investigation, Public Relations and Ethnic Group Relations, Court Organization and Procedure, and Courtroom Demeanor and Testifying. Jack began his career as a Jailer, a Dispatcher, and a Civil Deputy. By the time Vickie was born in 1967, Jack had advanced to Patrolman.

In 1968, construction on the Oroville Dam was complete,

and a dedication ceremony was part of the Big Dam Celebration Days scheduled over a five-day period, May 1-5. City planners arranged to have a carnival next to a boat and sport show in the Montgomery Ward parking lot, Miss Oroville and Little Miss Oroville pageants at various locations, wagon rides and public gold panning at Bedrock Park, open houses at local museums and the Chinese Temple, a historic art show and a fine arts show at Oroville High School, a parade and Dennis the Menace contest in Downtown Oroville, a traveling tent circus, banquets serving 300 guests inside the restaurant at Prospector's Village (along with poolside receptions), a honky-tonk party, a special train tour of the Dam site, old-time fiddlers in the park, a 36-hole golf tournament at Table Mountain Golf Course, and sailboats on Lake Oroville during the official dedication.

The event was advertised in newspapers throughout California and beyond. The local newspaper, the Oroville Mercury, released a special section about the Oroville Dam that was mailed to residents in all 50 states and in 22 foreign countries. Thousands of people were expected to stream into Oroville over the five-day celebratory period. Because of this, Jack, and other Butte County deputies, were put on around-the-clock duty. Oroville Police, the California Highway Patrol, and the California State Police were also in full force. Each was responsible for keeping things orderly and making sure visiting dignitaries and all the citizens remained safe.

The development of the Oroville Dam was due in thanks to the three previous California governors, Earl Warren (who at the time of the completion of the Oroville Dam was Chief Justice of the U.S. Supreme Court), Goodwin Knight, and Edmund Brown. However, recently elected Governor Ronald Reagan was the elected official chosen to speak at the dedication ceremony atop the Oroville Dam. This was exciting for spectators, not just because of the completion of the decades-long planning and construction of the dam, but because Ronald Reagan had been a famous Hollywood actor before devoting his life to politics.

Jack was thrilled that his job in law enforcement allowed him to be an active part of the celebration of the dam he and his dad helped to build, but he also found Reagan's visit to Oroville particularly interesting because of a character Reagan depicted in an acting role three years earlier. "Death Valley Days" was a popular television show about the Wild West, and in 1965, it featured an episode about Oatman, Arizona, the small mining town in which Jack was born. The television show told the story of the Oatman family, for whom the town was named, and the tragic story of how their wagons were attacked by a group of Apache Indians. Everyone was slaughtered except for two young girls who were kidnapped, held hostage, and later traded to a Mojave Indian tribe. Ronald Reagan played Lt. Col. Burke, of the U.S. military, who orchestrated the eventual capture of the only surviving daughter of the Oatman family, Olive.

Oatman, Arizona, eventually grew into a small, western town established close to gold mines near the Arizona and California border. Residents of the town were mostly miners who lived in shacks scattered along the hillsides. On a rare occasion, their families lived there as well, but the town

Above: Victoria and Smitty, circa 1930s

Right: Deputy Jack Smith, Paradise, Calif.

catered mostly to the miners and travelers passing through on Route 66.

Jack's parents, Smitty and Victoria, moved to Oatman, Arizona, in spring 1939 during the early stages of her pregnancy. On August 19, after a long, hot summer in one of the shacks on the hillside, Victoria gave birth to Jack. Oatman was also the small town in which Smitty abandoned his wife and infant son a few months later — prompting Victoria to return to her hometown of Fresno with her son. Despite the heartbreaking abandonment, however, during Jack's childhood, Victoria impressed upon him how special a place Oatman was to her because that's where she welcomed him into her arms.

Oatman was such a small town in Arizona that when Jack gave the name of his birthplace to others, very few people had heard of it. But Jack knew Ronald Reagan was familiar with Oatman, and it may have seemed menial to some, but Jack thought it was a big deal when Ronald Reagan arrived because there would be someone else in Oroville that day with connections to his birthplace.

On Saturday, May 4, 1968, day four of the Big Dam Celebration Days, Governor Reagan arrived in Oroville by helicopter. His wife, Nancy (a former Hollywood actress), and their children accompanied him. The helicopter landed at the top of the dam itself, and Reagan walked to a podium where he spoke in front of a crowd of 3,500. Reagan praised the Oroville Dam construction workers for their record-breaking achievement in moving more than 8 million cubic yards of earth and rock an average of 11 miles for the placement of the material in the 770-foot-high embankment—making it the tallest dam in the nation, a record that still exists today.

Reagan mentioned how the funding approval for the Oroville Dam had exposed the division between Northern and Southern Californians and how making the dam's completion was not just an engineering feat but a political accomplishment as well. He said the people of California were able to overcome a bitter north-south division by approving bonds for the project. Reagan said, "We are here today to dedicate more than a dam and a lake, we are here, in truth, to dedicate what is a memorial to the dedication, vision and hard work of many, many Californians whose love for their state has overcome any narrow sectionalism they may have felt."

The governor emphasized the importance of the Oroville Dam and the California State Water Project to all the people of California. He told the crowd, "California is doing what must be done toward preparing for the future. In fact, we have done more to help ourselves in the field of water development than all of the other states in the United States put together."

At first, Jack and numerous other law enforcement officers were assigned to the Oroville Dam site where Reagan gave his speech. Afterwards, when Reagan and his family were taken to Oroville's Municipal Auditorium for lunch, Jack was one of the officers assigned to keeping a safe space around the tables where the governor and his entourage were eating their lunch.

Later, as the luncheon was wrapping up, Jack was outside directing traffic in the front parking lot where the governor's helicopter awaited him and his family. When Reagan walked out of the Municipal Auditorium, Jack heard the governor tell the people he was with that he would be right back. A moment later, Jack looked up and was surprised to see the governor walking in his direction. Ronald Reagan approached Jack, shook his hand, thanked him for his service, and started a conversation. Maybe they talked about Oatman, maybe they talked about the Oroville Dam—only the two of them know. When asked about it later, Jack said, with a slight grin on his face, "Oh, we chatted for a bit."

Newspapers throughout California reported the events in the days and weeks leading up to the dedication of the Oroville Dam, the day of, and the days to follow. On Saturday, May 6, 1968, one of stories published by the *Oroville Mercury* newspaper featured a photo of a law enforcement officer surveilling the area near the table where Ronald Reagan and his family were sitting and eating lunch inside the Municipal Auditorium. Anyone reading the newspaper that day who had seen Jack in uniform as a jailer in the county jail, a bailiff in the courthouse, or a patrolman in the community would have instantly recognized him as the officer in the photo.

Jack stored important items in a safe place, including proof of identification such as his birth certificate and military service records, and sentimental items like the signet ring his mother gave him with his engraved initials, photos, and other memorabilia from his childhood, high school graduation, college, the Navy, and the police academy. But Jack also decided to clip a picture from the newspaper of Ronald Reagan's visit to Oroville and keep it as well. It wasn't, however, the photo with the officer near the Reagan family lunch table, but one of Ronald Reagan standing at the podium atop the Oroville Dam with Jack and his officers lined up in front. Jack didn't know what would become of Ronald Reagan's future, maybe he would go back into acting or possibly advance in his political career, but Jack wanted to keep a piece of memorabilia from his encounter with Ronald Reagan because of Reagan's association with Oatman, a place Jack's mother remembered fondly.

Little Jackie Smith Became...

CHAPTER FOUR
An Astute Lawman

Though Jack preferred simplicity in life, and he had a deep desire to help people, but he also had a thrill-seeking side, and he liked the ability to drive fast–safely. It just so happened that a career in law enforcement offered him both. There were slow work-shifts where the only excitement was helping an old lady across the street and the only pursuit was in the perfection of paperwork. At other times, there were urgent matters that required speeding with lights and siren — Code 3 calls. A few years into life as a deputy, Jack told his partner, Butch Ellis, a rookie at the time, that he hoped to one day respond to a call that would allow him to Code 3 through the Feather River Canyon — a 130 mile stretch of highway northeast of Oroville that twisted and turned through the mountains and where at high speeds drivers could get a rush of adrenaline while also taking a risk of crashing into wildlife or losing control of the vehicle and flying off a steep cliff.

One night, while Jack and Butch Ellis were on patrol, a call came in for a blood run — a request to quickly transport blood from the hospital in Oroville to the hospital in Chico, a town 25 miles away. After picking up the blood from Oroville Hospital, Jack told Ellis to buckle up. Seat belts weren't required at the time, so Ellis knew they were in for a ride — and he was right. Behind the wheel of a Dodge Monaco with a 440 CI engine, Jack turned on the lights and the siren then

Jack early 1970s

slammed on the gas pedal. Jack drove down the two lanes of Oro Dam Boulevard at 65 mph, and when they got to Highway 70, he turned northbound and gunned it. Ellis was belted at the waist, but his upper body was being thrown around so forcefully, he had to hold onto the shotgun attached to the car's dashboard.

Ellis was not new to speeding while in pursuit of another vehicle, but Jack was going faster than most cars and motorcycles Ellis was used to chasing. Ellis looked over at Jack and saw him with one hand on the steering wheel; the other hand held a lit cigarette, and Jack didn't appear nervous at all. Getting a little scared, Ellis asked him how fast he was going. Jack smiled and calmly said, "Ah, about 130." They were driving on a flat surface, but Ellis realized at that point he did not want to be in the passenger seat if Jack's call to Code 3 through the Feather River Canyon ever came.

By the early 1970s, Jack was promoted to detective. He was transferred out of Oroville to the sheriff's substation in the town of Paradise, a twenty-minute drive into the foothills north of Oroville where Jack's wide range of abilities in law enforcement earned him a reputation as one of the best deputies in the Butte County Sheriff's Department. He also enrolled in Butte College, a newly constructed community college located between Oroville and Paradise. Butte College had become the new location for the Feather River Police Academy, from which Jack graduated Basic Peace Officer Training in 1965. In addition to general education and electives, Jack took college-level courses in police science supervision, conference leading, sure plea systems, crime scene investigation and physical evidence, tear gas education, psychology, and he attended the Bahn Fair Institute of Scientific Law Enforcement at University of California, Davis. Because Ronald Reagan had been reelected for a second term as California governor, many of Jack's Certificates of Completion were signed by Reagan — adding even more of a special touch to them.

As a detective, Jack advanced to the rank of Sergeant and was transferred from Paradise to Gridley, a town located a short twenty-minute drive southwest of Oroville (where the population of the town was less than half of that in Oroville). Unlike the hills and mountains surrounding Paradise, Gridley was in the agricultural flatland of Southeastern Butte County, at the northern tip of the Sacramento Valley. Because of his new location, Jack took additional college courses that would make him more proficient at the agricultural-related aspects his job; this included Livestock Rustling and Livestock Theft Patrol and Investigation; he also took Spanish language classes so he could more adequately support the increasing number of Spanish-speaking people in the community. In addition, even though Jack was an airplane mechanic in the Navy, to better assist in the event of an emergency involving crop dusters, he took a college course in aeronautics.

In Gridley, most of Jack's investigative work involved domestic disturbances, neighbor disputes, assaults, bar brawls, burglaries, auto accidents with pedestrians, cyclists, and trains, drunk driving arrests, stabbings, accidental and intentional shootings, and drownings in local ponds, creeks, and rivers. By the early 1970s, many people in Butte County were aware of Jack's exceptional work, and once he was transferred to Gridley, he began receiving formal recognition of his skill at a local, inter-county, inter-departmental, and a national level.

One Sunday afternoon, shortly after Jack transferred to the Gridley substation, a woman called for Oroville Ambulance to come to her home on Highway 70 because her estranged husband shot himself in front of her house. When the ambulance arrived, a bloodied gunman ran from the front of the house into a nearby field where he turned back and fired two shots at the paramedics. Bill Scott, of Oroville Ambulance, requested assistance from the Butte County Sheriff's Department.

Within minutes, Jack and three other deputies arrived at the residence while two California Highway Patrol units stopped traffic on the highway. The deputies saw a man holding a .22 caliber rifle in a field near the house. Based on information they were given, the officers knew the man was the woman's estranged husband; he showed up at her house and wanted to talk, and when she refused, he asked their four-year-old daughter to come outside and see him. In front of the young child, the man shot himself in the chest. From what the deputies knew, the man's rifle had a magazine capacity of 11 rounds — of which they believed at least three had been used (one on himself and two at the paramedics).

The injured gunman started walking back toward the house, but when he spotted the sheriff deputy's car slowly moving toward him, he returned to the field. Deputy Butler was behind the wheel of the patrol car, and Jack was in the passenger's seat using the PA system attempting to talk the gunman into dropping the rifle. Deputies Hageman and Sumner walked behind the car. Instead of surrendering to the officers, however, the injured and distraught man aimed the rifle at the deputies and put his finger on the trigger. Rather than continue to confront the man, all the deputies retreated with the car to a secure place behind a barn.

The gunman stood in the field for a short time, then started walking toward the barn, where the deputies were waiting. When he got within 25 feet of the barn, Jack suddenly appeared in the field near him. Jack wasn't wearing any protective gear, but he got close enough to ask the gunman if he could talk to him. The gunman agreed to talk but kept his gun at ready. As they talked, Jack gradually walked closer to the man. When Jack got within 10 feet, the gunman told him to stop. Jack stopped walking, but kept the conversation going.

Jack didn't want to be shot, but he also knew the man was suicidal, and he knew all too well the pain and confusion the man's daughter would experience if he was to commit suicide, so in the field with the distraught man bleeding from a self-inflicted gunshot wound, Jack maintained a calm persona and continued talking. A short time later, the gunman dropped the weapon and allowed Jack to retrieve it. The gunman was then taken to the hospital for treatment of his injuries, both physical and psychological. When asked later about what he said to the gunman, Jack simply said, "Oh, I just sat and talked to him for a while."

Jack was commended for his courage and bravery by fellow officers Sumner and Butler, and he was formally recognized by Captain Leroy Wood. Ironically, five months later, the Butte County Sheriff's Department sent Jack to a 37-hour training course in Dispute Crisis Intervention.

Jack's exceptional work ethic was also acknowledged by law enforcement officials in other departments, one example of which was indicated in a letter written by a Lieutenant with the California Highway Patrol to Sheriff Larry Gillick:

> Once again you and a member of your department have earned our expression of appreciation for your assistance. Deputy Jack Smith of your Gridley Substation was the first officer at the scene of a major injury accident on Oro-Gridley Road at Larkin Road on July 1st. He

immediately took charge, protecting the scene, caring for the injured and securing names and addresses of witnesses prior to our arrival. The professional manner in which Deputy Smith handled the situation reflects credit certainly on him as well as you and your training programs. Thank you.

A short time later, Jack received the following letter:

On behalf of the Sheriff Roy Whitaker and the Sutter County Sheriff's Department Detective Division, please accept our sincere appreciation for your splendid assistance to the detectives of this department during the investigation of the...narcotic investigation. Your assistance made a difficult task much easier. Once again, our sincere thanks, and our pledge to return to the assistance at any available opportunity.

On August 31, 1973, a motorist driving in a rural area on the outskirts of Oroville saw women's clothing strewn about in the brush near the street. Two Butte County Deputies, Michael Yugo and Perry Reniff, responded to the call and after a search of the area, a woman's body was discovered in a shallow creek. Officers also found tire marks, a faint footprint, and marks on the ground that indicted the woman had likely been dragged to the water's edge. When neighbors were questioned, someone reported seeing an unfamiliar

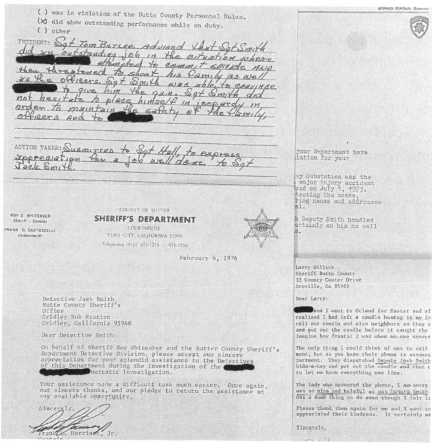

Documents pertaining to the law enforcement duties of Jack L. Smith

white vehicle in the area the night before.

The *Oroville Mercury* Newspaper reported that the wo-man had been hogtied with twine and strangled. The woman was naked except for a red handkerchief around her neck, and local news reported a pile of clothes were found neatly stacked on the ground near the creek – a black and white chiffon dress, a short white jacket, and white shoes.

No identifying information could be found on the victim or in the area, so her photograph was sent to newspapers and television stations in the area, and local police and deputies carried her picture while questioning people they had contact with during routine interactions with the community. Her identity was eventually revealed when a report from the California Department of Justice matched the victim's fingerprints to that of a fifty-four-year old woman named Helen Gould from Gridley – the same town in which Jack was stationed as a detective.

The victim was buried the following week, and the investigation into her death continued. Deputies claimed the murder, having occurred on a Friday of a three-day weekend combined with too much information being leaked to the public, had hampered the investigation. Then, on September 12, an arrest was made – a thirty-nine-year-old man named Charles Sellers, an unemployed vocational nurse and neighbor of the victim. He appeared in court on September 17, where he entered an innocent plea to first-degree murder. Sellers could not afford an attorney, so he was referred to the Office of the Public Defender, and a preliminary hearing was scheduled for October 1.

At 2 A.M. on the morning of October 1, a deputy at the Butte County Jail heard a weak voice calling for help and found Charles Sellers on the floor of his cell; he was surrounded by blood and too weak to sit up. Sellers had attempted suicide by cutting himself on the inside of his left arm with a razor blade. He was taken to the hospital and treated and then returned to the jail. Later that afternoon,

Sellers appeared in court where he entered a guilty plea to the charge of second-degree murder. Sentencing was scheduled for October 19, allowing time for the probation department to investigate and report on Sellers' prior criminal history.

By the time of the sentencing hearing, investigators were informed that Charles Sellers had been committed twice to the Atascadero State Hospital, once in 1958 for a term of 16 months after sexual abuse of an eight-year old boy. At that time, Sellers was labeled a sexual psychopath. Five weeks after Sellers' release from the state hospital in 1960, he committed sexual acts with an eleven-year old girl. He was returned to Atascadero State Prison, where the medical director deemed him a menace to the health and safety to others. Sellers was sentenced to prison and released on parole seven years before killing Helen Gould.

Though the case may have seemed to be clear-cut and appear to play itself out on the pages of the local newspapers, there was much more going on behind the scenes with specific law enforcement officers — specifically Jack — but few people outside of the Butte County Sheriff's Department knew that. It wasn't until the Helen Gould murder investigation attracted the attention of writers for a national crime detective magazine, *Master Detective*, that locals were more fully informed about the deputy who solved the case.

At the time of the Helen Gould's death, Jack worked as a detective at the Butte County Sheriff's substation in Gridley, the town in which both the victim and the perpetrator lived. The local newspaper, the Gridley Herald, mentioned the story on several occasions; Jack's name appeared in the newspaper when the arrest of Charles Sellers was announced and when Captain Leroy Wood told reporters he sent Sgt. Jack Smith to pick up Charles Sellers from his home and transport him to the Sheriff's Station. The reality, however, was that Jack was much more involved than that—in fact, upon news of the discovery of Helen Gould's dead body, Captain Leroy Wood told Jack, "…this is your case. Don't work on anything else until you come up with something on this one."

With Jack at the helm, there was no hampering of the case due to a three-day weekend, as later reported in the news, because Jack began his investigation immediately, and he worked tirelessly from that point on. Using a tape recorder and notepad, Jack interviewed Mrs. Gould's friends, family, and neighbors and began running background checks. One young relative was the last known person to have seen Mrs. Gould alive. The relative visited Mrs. Gould around 7 P.M. on the night of her disappearance and noticed that she was wearing a dress, unlike the pants she usually wore. The relative asked her why she was dressed up. He said she laughed and told him, "I'm going to go out tonight and get in trouble."

Gould was known as a friendly person, but reportedly never one to pick up a man. A close friend of Mrs. Gould said, "If she had a dress on the night she disappeared, you can be sure she had a date with someone she knew and trusted. She wouldn't go out with a stranger."

Local automotive businesses and hardware stores were contacted in hopes of tracing the electrical wire used to bind the victim. No one was familiar with the wire. All cars belonging to people connected with the case were inspected, but no similar wire was found. Jack also went to the victim's apartment on numerous occasions. He collected various items from her apartment, including a note which read, "Hi Babe. See you later. Love you too."

Mrs. Gould was married but separated, so naturally Jack questioned her estranged husband. He said he had not been in contact with his wife for quite some time and that two friends were with him watching movies on the night his wife was murdered; the husband's alibi was later confirmed. Jack also questioned neighbors, one of whom told him that another neighbor, Charles Sellers, known as Chuck, was married but that he once bragged about being intimate with Mrs. Gould. The neighbor said he had seen Helen Gould and Chuck leave notes for each other on her mailbox. Chuck drove a white Chevy Buick, a description similar to that of the vehicle seen in the area of the crime the night before the body was discovered. The neighbor told Jack that Chuck's car had a loud muffler and was heard leaving the area on the night Mrs. Gould disappeared.

Jack immediately questioned Chuck and his wife, Naomi. Both were cooperative. Chuck told Jack he was home the night Helen Gould disappeared and that he and his wife were watching television. Chuck specifically mentioned watching *The Dean Martin Show*, a popular comedy-variety television series on a regular season schedule at the time.

Jack noticed a lot of prescription bottles in Chuck and Naomi's residence. There were also a lot of empty beer cans. Jack asked about both. The couple said they took the prescription pills for their ailments and that the beers were night caps. Jack asked Chuck if he drove his car anywhere on the night Gould disappeared. Chuck replied, "No, and my wife can verify that. That might have been the night that I drove it from the street into the garage about 4:30 P.M., but I didn't drive it anywhere else."

Jack decided against any further questioning at that time. When the background check showed that Chuck had twice been committed to a state mental institution for sexual offenses, and when a check with local television stations confirmed *The Dean Martin Show* was not on television at the time Chuck and his wife had indicated, Chuck was asked to take a polygraph. He complied. Unfortunately, the exam was inconclusive because Chuck said he was under the effects of medication due to headaches he'd been having. Chuck was told he would be examined again when he wasn't taking any medication. He agreed.

At the time of the Gould murder investigation, Jack had just turned thirty-three years old. He had lived twenty-two of those years without answers to many questions he had about his mother's death, so he was going to do everything he could to prevent others from living with that type of uncertainty about their love one. Of course, Jack wanted to get a murderer off the street to protect the community, but he also wanted to make sure the numerous family and friends of Helen Gould could get the answers they needed for closure.

Chuck became the primary suspect. If he wasn't the murderer, Jack was certain the answers he was seeking could be found from someone else in the apartment complex or the neighborhood. Jack started showing up at Helen Gould's apartment complex at all hours of the day and night. There were times he sat in a chair on the patio and smoked a cigarette in plain view of all the apartment complex tenants. Other times, Jack sat on a curb in front of the apartment complex and talked to people walking by. Sometimes he spent hours sitting on Mrs. Gould's apartment staircase or walking up and down them. Occasionally, Jack would knock on different doors in the apartment complex and ask if someone had called the police. Jack kept himself visible and waited for someone to break.

In the meantime, funeral services were held for Helen Gould. Newspaper reports indicated she worked at a local cannery and was survived by two sisters, a son, and two grandchildren. Also included in the local news was information about a continued investigation into her murder, some of which had been intentionally given incorrectly in order to mislead the public to help weed-out false leads — for example, the suspected cause of death was listed as strangulation instead of drowning and that her clothes were neatly folded, as opposed to the reality that they were strewn about.

Nearly two weeks after Helen Gould's murder, Chuck Sellers and his wife, Naomi, got into an argument. Chuck told Naomi he was going to shut her up just like he shut up Helen. Naomi asked her husband if he killed Gould. He said, "Yes, I did. And you keep your mouth shut."

After confessing the murder to his wife, Chuck went into the bathroom. Naomi quietly called the Sheriff's Department.

Jack responded to the call and when Naomi answered the door, she was hysterical. In a confident manner and gentle voice, Jack assured Naomi that everything was going to be alright, and it calmed her down.

When Chuck emerged from the bathroom, Jack asked him to come to headquarters for further questioning. Chuck agreed. In the meantime, Naomi was given a polygraph. She told officers that her husband had been unable to sleep and became nervous each time he saw "Sergeant Smith" around the apartment complex, and he immediately took a tranquilizer.

Chuck proclaimed his innocence to law enforcement and took the polygraph. He was then informed that his answers indicated he had knowledge of, or had participated in, the murder of Helen Gould. Chuck continued to maintain his innocence, but a short time later he broke down crying. He complained that he had little sleep and was edgy whenever he saw Sergeant Smith "prowling about." That edginess led to an argument with his wife and the threat to her life.

Chuck admitted to making a big mistake; he then confessed to killing Helen Gould and described the details of his crime. Jack was relieved that Helen Gould's family would finally get answers to some of the questions they had about the tragic loss of a loved one, something he often hoped for himself. Jack also realized from this case that answers sometimes led to even more questions. For example, Chuck Sellers initially claimed he killed Gould because he feared she was going to tell his wife about their sexual relationship, but he later said he killed her, "Because I didn't like her laugh." Charles Sellers was sentenced to five years-to-life in state prison.

At the sentencing hearing, the judge asked Charles Sellers' attorney if he had anything to say. He said there really wasn't much to say because of "...certain inescapable facts in this case."

The disturbing details and unusual cause of the murder combined with the exceptional law enforcement work on the case led to Sergeant Jack Smith being featured in the 1975 edition of the nationally distributed *Master Detective Magazine*. Placed at the top of the cover page of the magazine was the title "Riddle of the Hogtied Nude in the Creek."

When family and friends found out about Jack being featured in the magazine, they complimented his work, but Jack, not one to draw attention to himself, remained humble. He didn't show the magazine to many people. In fact, when asked about it later, Jack didn't take credit for doing anything extraordinary in the investigation—he felt it was relatively simple to explain. After seeing the pill bottles and beer cans in Chuck and his wife's home during his first interview with them, Jack intended to drive Chuck to drink because, Jack later said, "The drunk man speaks the sober man's truth."

By this time in Jack's life, he had purchased a new hardcover Samsonite suitcase. The old Samsonite with his initials on a plate near the handle, which he received as a high school graduation gift from his dad and stepmother, was being used for Jack's memorabilia. In addition to the signet ring his mother gave him, his birth certificate, his certificate of baptism, pictures of him from his childhood, some with his mother that were given to him by his Aunt Grace, other family photos, his high school yearbook, his Navy records, and a newspaper clipping from Ronald Reagan's visit to Oroville in 1968, Jack added certificates of completion in law enforcement, letters of recognition and achievement in various areas of law enforcement – and in 1975 a few copies of the *Master Detective Magazine* were also placed in the Samsonite.

Little Jackie Smith Became…

CHAPTER FIVE
A Gentleman

Prior to a career in law enforcement, Butte County Sheriff Larry Gillick had been a semi-professional baseball pitcher. When Gillick was elected as county sheriff, he preferred to not carry a gun because he worried that he might hurt someone. Instead, one night, while a fellow officer shined a flashlight on a crime suspect running from officers, Gillick picked up a rock, took aim, and pitched that rock directly into the suspect's back. The suspect dropped to the ground and was detained. Gillick's technique continued to be effective time and time again, and even after he became Butte County Sheriff, Gillick still refused to carry a gun. When Sheriff Gillick retired, reporters asked him why he never carried a gun. He replied, "I thought I might hurt someone; I always figured I could do better with a pocketful of rocks."

Jack worked under the leadership of Sheriff Gillick. Indeed, Jack carried a gun, but like Gillick, he preferred to not use it. Also, like Gillick, Jack brought his own unique strengths to the department that made him less likely to use a gun. Jack didn't have the same pitching arm as Gillick, but he was kind, respectful and compassionate to everyone he encountered — this made him effective in de-escalating chaotic situations. Butte County Sheriff's Department dispatcher Mary Jane Perrucci described Jack as the type of officer who would get out of his car and meet people in the community. When asked about it later, Mary Jane said, "We knew which officers would go on a call and all hell would break loose. Jack was not one of them. He was calm. I loved and respected him because of the way he treated people and because he never compromised his principles."

Some of Jack's colleagues at the Sheriff's Department referred to him as "Gentleman Jack" (a comical and ironic reference to the whiskey, considering Jack rarely consumed alcohol). The reference to Jack being a gentleman was not a new one. Many years earlier, when Jack was seventeen-years old, an Oroville High School English teacher wrote in Jack's yearbook, "You were always a gentleman and a good student."

Jack's children, however, had their own way of describing their dad — he was a lot like a man they saw on TV. When Jack became a deputy in 1965, *The Andy Griffith Show* was one of the top-rated television programs, but it went off the air in 1968. Because, however, reruns were shown in black and white and in color, Alan and Vickie spent their elementary school years entertained by the characters portrayed by Andy Griffith, Don Knotts, Ron Howard, and others. Most intriguing to Alan and Vickie, however, was how similar their dad was to the show's main character, Andy Taylor of Mayberry. There were slight physical resemblances between Jack and the actor, Andy Griffith, such as their height and physical build, some of the facial features, and the ear-to-ear smile, but it was the mannerisms of the fictional character Andy Griffith played that resonated with them the most — for example, the way Andy Taylor fathered his son, Opie. Like Jack, Andy Taylor of Mayberry was a gentle, nurturing father who spent

he didn't. One example of this was described in a letter sent to Sheriff Larry Gillick:

> Dear Larry:
>
> ...and I went to Orland for Easter and after arriving there, I realized I had left a candle burning in my front room. I tried to call our cousin and also neighbors so they could get my hid-a-key and put out the candle before it caught the house on fire. You can imagine how frantic I was when no one answered.
>
> The only thing I could think of was to call the Biggs Police Department, but as you known their phone is answered by the Sheriff's Department. They dispatched Deputy Jack Smith to my house to get the hide-a-key and put out the candle and then called me back in Orland to let me know everything was fine.
>
> The lady who answered the phone, I am sorry, I didn't get her name, was so nice and helpful as was Deputy Smith. They didn't act like it was a dumb thing to do even though I felt like it when I called.
>
> Please thank them again for me and I want to let you know how much I appreciated their kindness. It certainly made our day a very nice one.

Beginning in the early stages of his career in law enforcement, Jack was known for developing relationships of mutual respect with some of the inmates at the county jail. One night when a burglar alarm went off at the Western Pacific Headquarters, Jack responded to the call and arrested the burglar. The suspect's background was run, and Jack discovered the man had escaped custody in Ohio ten years earlier and had been on the run and riding the train rails ever since. The burglar was a skilled locksmith, so while waiting for authorities in Ohio to transport him back to their custody, he helped Jack pick locks on confiscated items from crime scenes. In the end, the burglar was not returned to Ohio, and after serving his time for burglary in the Butte County Jail, he was a free man. Before the man left the jail, he told everyone how appreciative he was of the way Jack treated him.

Ann's younger brother, Rick, described Jack as the type of person who "treated everyone the same whether it was his best friend or a drunk on the street" — and it was regardless of gender, race, ethnicity, social status, or background. This earned Jack a reputation in the community as being a fair cop which came in handy during situations where unfamiliar or less friendly officers may not have been comfortable. Race relations in Oroville had become less friendly since Jack was in high school, and an increase of incidents involving racism and hostility against racial minorities created a lack of respect and trust by people in minority communities toward some of the people in the Caucasian community — and, at times, toward law enforcement, as well.

One night when Jack was still a patrolman, a call came in for officers to report to a bar brawl in a predominantly African

American community in Oroville known as Cadillac Flats. It was Jack, a Caucasian law enforcement officer, and a patrol-man from the Oroville Police Department, also Caucasian, who responded first to the call. When they arrived, Jack started to walk into the bar. The Oroville police officer wanted to wait for backup. As Jack advanced toward the front door of the bar, the police officer said, "Jack, if you go in there, you're the stupidest person I know."

Jack looked back at the officer, smiled, and walked inside anyway. By the time the other officers arrived, the situation was under control. Butch Ellis, one of Jack's patrol partners, later said of Jack, "He had a way of dealing with people. He was one of the coolest guys I knew, the officer many others wanted to emulate. A lot of guys listened to every word he said. I always knew I was with one of the best when I was with Jack."

Jack's status as a respectful officer extended to youth in the community. He was a loving father with his own children, and he used this approach to relate to the younger people in the community. One evening, Jack was driving his patrol car with Deputy Butch Ellis in the passenger seat when they spotted a group of teenagers hanging around the drive-in theater after business hours. Jack pulled up his car to the group and walked up to the teens. A couple of the young men greeted Jack by hugging him. Later, Jack and Ellis were having coffee at Thrifty Diner when Jack started searching all around him. He told Ellis, "I lost my mace to one of my asshole buddies."

Ellis wanted to go back to the drive-in theater to find the

teens right then, but Jack wanted to wait. By the time Jack and Ellis started their shift together the following night, Jack had his mace back. When he was off duty earlier in the day, he found the boys, and he simply asked for it. They returned it and apologized. When asked about the incident later, Ellis said, "It came down to respect. Jack gave people chances. He wasn't there to make an arrest. When Jack needed to, he would put someone against the wall and tell them to knock it off, and they did it. But it didn't always come to that."

Even in his personal life, Jack's ability to earn the trust of and communicate effectively with young people was recognized and utilized. When Jack's mother-in-law, Carine, lost a family member in a car accident, she asked Jack to break the news to Ann's youngest brother, Kevin, because they knew the death of the loved one would impact Kevin more than Ann's other siblings. Kevin was not yet ten years old when Jack sat him down, gave him the heartbreaking news, answered all his questions, and helped calm his fears and sadness.

Beginning in late June 1974, Butte County Deputies joined nearby counties on a manhunt for a 6' 2," 240-pound murder and kidnapping suspect named John Card. Card, a wood cutter, stabbed and strangled a veterinarian and his thirteen-year old daughter. He kidnapped the veterinarian's wife and son, then forced the wife to withdraw $5,000 in cash from the bank before shooting and killing her; the veterinarian's son escaped and notified authorities. John Card's crime spree put law enforcement agencies from Butte and neighboring counties on high alert. John Card then kidnapped a widow and her two children; holding them hostage, he drove them into three other states and then back to northern California. Five days later, John Card chained the widow and her two children to a tree in a campground and left them; they escaped a short time later. On July 4th, the car John Card was driving was seen parked at a celebration near Truckee in Northern California. He was arrested without incident in possession of weapons and $3,000 cash.

A few days later, just as Butte County Deputies were settling back into a slower-paced routine of lower-level crimes, they were back on a manhunt again, and it began on July 8, 1974, when a 47-year old woman was traveling northbound on Highway 70, twenty miles south of Oroville. At 9 P.M., she picked up two young-adult, male hitchhikers. Immediately after getting into her car, the young men threatened the woman with a gun and forced her to drive them toward the small community of Honcut and onto an unpaved portion of Dunstone Road. There, the young men forced the woman out of her car and smashed her head with a rock. They drove away in the woman's Datsun sedan and $5,300 in cash she had in her purse. A short time later, the young men turned around and went back to where the woman was laying on the ground. One of the young men pulled out a gun and shot her in the head, then they drove off and left her to die.

The woman regained consciousness sometime later and began to crawl along the dirt road. By the next morning, after alternating between crawling and walking a 5-6 miles distance, she finally reached the back door of a residence.

There, a man helped the injured woman inside and called emergency services. Butte County deputies and an ambulance responded. The woman was surprisingly coherent and able to describe her assailants and the events of her ordeal. She was taken to the hospital where she underwent surgery to remove a bullet from her brain.

An all-points bulletin was put out for two young men, approximately nineteen years old, along with the physical descriptions given to them by the injured woman. The next day, the victim's car was found abandoned in a ditch, and officers said they had additional clues about the suspects — one was a seventeen-year old from Gridley, the other was a seventeen-year old from Biggs, a rural community four miles north of Gridley. Both belonged to the community near the Sheriff's substation in Gridley where Jack was stationed.

On July 11th, Sheriff's Deputies arrested the Gridley teen at a local motel. His accomplice, the Biggs teen, was officially named and a manhunt was on. The Biggs youth was believed to be driving to Reno in a blue or green 1963 or 1964 Mercury Comet. Two days later, the Bigg's youth was arrested in Idaho. Butte County Deputies began extradition talks, and plans were discussed for how they were going to transport the teen, presumed dangerous and a potential flight risk, back to Butte County.

Members of the community wanted to know how and when the teenage suspect was going to be returned to Butte County and held responsible for his senseless crime. On July 18th, the *Oroville Mercury* newspaper told the community under a headline titled, "Biggs Youth Being Returned," who exactly would be flying to Caldwell, Idaho, to bring back the second of two seventeen-year old suspects wanted in the shooting of the forty-seven-year old woman – it was Sergeant Jack Smith.

Trials were scheduled for the crimes against the woman and another victim, a man they were found to have assaulted and robbed two months earlier. The Gridley teen testified in court that he felt bad about what they did to the woman, so before he was arrested at the motel, he attempted to visit his victim when she was in the hospital, but he wasn't allowed in her room. Despite his remorse, the Gridley teen was convicted of six felonies and sentenced to prison. Sadly, before the trial of the Bigg's teen began, the forty-seven-year old woman died of a heart attack. This complicated the second trial, but in the end, the Biggs teen was convicted and sentenced as well.

Despite being a friendly, laid-back, community-centered man with a strong grip on his moral compass and "ah shucks!" similarities to Sheriff Andy Taylor of Mayberry, in the mid-1970s, nearing the age of forty, Jack would learn first-hand that not everyone cared about how nice he was or how captivating of smile he had — particularly desperate criminals out for some easy cash.

Whenever possible, Jack preferred working the night shift. Even when he wasn't on the clock, he liked to stick to the nocturnal schedule. One morning, about 1:30 A.M. when Jack was off duty, he was traveling through Sutter County, south of Butte County. He was running low on cigarettes, as he entered the town of Yuba City, 30 miles southwest of Oroville, so he decided to stop at a convenience store he knew was open late at night.

Because Jack was not working, he wore civilian clothes and drove his personal vehicle when he parked in front of the Jiffy Food Store. He had no idea that two men entered the market a few minutes earlier. One of the men picked beer out of the cooler and took it to the counter. While the store's assistant manager, working alone that night, was waiting for the man at the counter to finish counting his change, the man near the front door pulled out a handgun. Both men demanded all the money in the cash register. Before the assistant manager could respond, however, they saw headlights and Jack's car pulled into a parking space. The man at the door hid the gun inside his coat.

Jack entered the store and greeted the man at the door; the man responded by pulling his gun out, pointing it at Jack, and ordering him to stand near the assistant manager. Jack had had guns pointed at him more than once while on duty, including the man he talked into giving up the gun in the middle of a field, and it wasn't his first time while off the clock either. One night, after working late when Alan was a toddler and Vickie was an infant, Jack attempted to sneak into his house, hoping not to wake anyone. He was met with the barrel of a gun – his wife, Ann, was on the trigger end.

Regardless of his experience, however, Jack was caught off-guard as he entered the convenience store. Still, his calm instinct kicked in, and Jack did as he was told. He stood next to the assistant manager while the robbers took the cash from the register drawer; they also ordered Jack to give them any money he had. Jack handed over his wallet and checkbook and tried to rationalize with the men, but they had their minds set, and they wanted nothing to do with a man off the street telling them what they should and should not be doing. Jack was then forced to walk in front of both men with the gun pointed at his back. The assistant manager remained near the cash register, as Jack and the two robbers exited the store.

Once outside, Jack was told to walk away slowly. He did. When Jack noticed the men had run in the opposite direction, he rushed to his car, retrieved his service revolver from beneath the driver's seat, and began to chase the men on foot. When the men were in sight, Jack fired a round at the ground near them in hopes that fear would make them stop. It didn't. The men jumped a fence and escaped. They made off with $20-$40 from the register, $68 in cash from Jack's wallet as well as his credit cards and checkbook. The following day, the local newspaper reported the robbery under the title, "Deputy Chases YC Robbers."

The men were described in the newspaper as being in their late teens to early twenties, one about 6'3" and the other about 5'11." The shorter of the two was said to have had shag-style brown hair and buck teeth. The men knew Jack's name, address, and if they read the newspaper the following day, they knew he worked as a Butte County deputy.

For a while, Jack kept an eye out for them in the area around his home but never saw them. To the best of his knowledge, the men were never caught. Jack simply added one more newspaper clipping to the growing collection in his Samsonite.

Little Jackie Smith Became...

CHAPTER SIX
A Modest Man

Jack's high school yearbook was filled with comments about how his friends, schoolmates, teachers, and other school staff felt about him; he was referred to as a real sweet guy, a nice guy, a swell guy, a swell kid, a fine guy, and a real wonderful boy. Teenage Jack was described as someone who had a knack for making people happy. It was recommended that Jack, "Stay as nice as you are, and you will go far."

Throughout high school, Jack was an average student academically, but was very good at athletics. His classmates complimented him as a great baseballer, a bowling buddy, a swimming pal, and someone who could really play water polo. One classmate joked by addressing Jack as "Hercules" and another jokingly stated, "To Jack 'Mr. America' Smith, lots of luck to the hunkhead who broke our torso tester in PE."

In Jack's 1957 high school yearbook, classmates commented on what a great teammate he was, and later, as a deputy in the sixties and seventies, Jack was still referred to in similar terms. Over the years, he had proven himself to be a team player who never accepted credit for anything he didn't deserve—and because he was rather shy, Jack was reluctant to accept commendation even when it was well deserved. In fact, Jack's colleagues enjoyed teasing him about his shy and conservative nature. One example of this occurred after photos were taken of Jack when he and another officer were

No. _____

Name _Jack Smith_

Order _____

Remarks _Porno_

Retouched _____

Order Finished _7-12-74_

Reorder _____

Reorder _____

Getting dressed after Tom Butler & I had gone swimming in a creek south-west of Howcut & recovered a pistol used in a armed robbery, kidnaps, rape case. Tom located the weapon

searching for a weapon they believed was used in the commission of a crime. A few days after the search, a large manila envelope was left for Jack at the Butte County Sheriff's station in Gridley. Inside the envelope titled "Porno" was an

Jack shirtless by creek

8x10, black and white photo. Jack was the only person in the picture. He was standing with his rear-end propped against the hood of a squad car and leaning forward to tie his boot.

The car was parked on a dirt road with tall, dried grass and old wooden fence posts in the background. Jack was wearing only a pair of pants and his boots, no shirt or any upper-body portion of his uniform. Jack happened to look up from his forward-leaning position just as the photographer snapped the picture.

Jack never wanted to appear indecent, including with his attire. His own children rarely saw him without his signature plaid shirt over a white, v-nick undershirt neatly tucked into pants, so Jack would only have been caught on camera without a shirt if he was hard at work—and his colleagues knew this. Jack got a good laugh at the joke, and intended to keep the photo and the envelope, however, he worried that someone unfamiliar with the true nature of the photo might see it someday, so before storing the photo in his Samsonite suitcase, Jack wrote on the outside of the envelope:

> Getting dressed after Tom Butler and I had gone swimming in a creek South-west of Honcut and recovered a pistol used in an armed robbery, kidnap, rape case.

Always one to give credit where credit was due, Jack added, "Tom located the weapon."

By 1976, Jack had joined the Butte County Search and Rescue Team, and it was there that he experienced the discomfort of being singled out for the success of a team effort. On Wednesday, February 4, two men were reported missing in the mountains near Feather Falls, a 410' waterfall,

25 miles northeast of Oroville in the Plumas National Forest of the Sierra Nevada Mountain Range. The men were identified as twenty-two-year old Bill Adams from Los Angeles and nineteen-year old Ron Wood of Oroville. The pair were reportedly last seen at 3 A.M. when they left a party driving in Ron Wood's truck. Deputies searched the snow-covered area until late Thursday night but found nothing. The Butte County Search and Rescue Coordinator was Lt. Ken Mickelson; Jack was the co-coordinator. They wanted to put a helicopter in the air, but high winds made that too dangerous.

Bills Adams had come to the Oroville area three weeks earlier as part of the production crew for a film titled *Alamo Charlie*. Bill Adams' father, Elmo Adams, was a member of the movie production crew as well and became concerned when he had not heard from his son, who otherwise stayed in close contact. Adams had several hundred dollars in cash on him, so foul play was a consideration. Ron Wood was a local man who worked for a fence company in Oroville. The Search and Rescue team consisted of 12-15 deputies and several civilian volunteers including Elmo Adams and Bill Adams' brother, Thomas Adams, a paramedic from Sacramento.

With no luck on Thursday, search teams set out again at daybreak on Friday. Two helicopters joined them later in the day. By 5 P.M., Ron Wood's truck was found on the side of an embankment. Footprints of two men, presumably Bill Adams and Ron Wood, and canine footprints, possibly Ron Wood's dog, were seen leaving the area. The search team followed the footprints until one set, along with the dog's prints, went into one direction and disappeared.

Deputies followed the other set of footprints for approximately two miles before finding a shirt lying on the ground. A short distance away, they found another shirt. The search continued until the lifeless body of nineteen-year old Ron Wood was discovered. He had apparently begun to suffer from hypothermia, stripped himself of his clothes and while attempting to climb a hillside, he slipped, fell, and his head struck a rock. Thomas Adams, brother of the other missing man, found Ron Wood's body, but he remained optimistic that his brother was still alive.

The next morning, Saturday, the ground search and rescue team continued its efforts in the cold, rugged mountains. They found footprints on several occasions that went in circles, but they would eventually disappear. As the evening approached, the search team became concerned that Bill Adams may not survive another night in 20-degree temperatures, and then, just as Lt. Ken Mickelson was planning to call off the search for the night, he received a radio call—Jack and another member of the Search and Rescue Team found tracks of a man and a dog. Jack wanted to continue searching into the night. Lt. Mickelson agreed.

Other search and rescue units joined Jack and his partner in "leap-frogging" at 5400 feet elevation through thick brush, rough terrain, deep snow, and in the dark of night. Sometimes the four-wheel drive vehicles got stuck, so the search team resumed on foot with flashlights. The tracks of the man and canine were difficult to follow because the snow had been melting, and they intertwined with bear tracks and bear hunter tracks.

At 11 P.M., searchers heard the barking of a dog and the sound of a person whistling. As the searchers approached, they found Bill Adams and the dog huddled in the brush. Searchers had been warned that the dog may be aggressive and expected they might have to shoot him, but they didn't because the first words out of Bill Adams' mouth were, "Don't shoot my dog."

An ambulance with a doctor was requested to meet the search team near Feather Falls so they could transport Bill Adams to Oroville Hospital. Adams was wearing jeans, motorcycle boots, and a goose-down jacket his brother, Thomas, had given him. He suffered from exposure, shock, hypothermia, and severe frostbite to his feet. Adams described his ability to survive by staying awake to keep his mind active and to stay by the logging roads. He also said he pretended he had been captured by hostile Native Americans and instead of killing him they would make him a blood brother if he could survive the ordeal.

Bill Adams was reunited with his father and brother. The following day, Adams' mother visited him in the hospital. He told the story of how he and Ron Wood were at a party, and at 11 P.M., Bill Adams went to sleep in Ron Wood's truck. At 3A.M., Ron Wood woke Bill and asked him to drive back to Oroville because he had been drinking and didn't feel like it would be safe for him to drive. Ron Wood fell asleep on the drive, snow was falling, Bill Adams took a wrong turn, and at some point, the truck went off the road and down an embankment. The two men started walking but they separated because Bill Adams believed they were going in the wrong direction. Bill Adams did not know why the dog chose to go with him instead of with his owner, Ron Wood. Adams said the company of Ron Wood's dog helped him stay alive, and he was hoping to keep him.

The rescue team estimated that Bill Adams had walked 40 miles in the snow-covered backcountry for four days without food or sleep. He later told reporters he had met several people during his time in the mountains, but didn't know if they were real or not. Adams said he walked up to some of the people, but they turned into snowmen. He also said he walked up to a trailer, and it turned into snow.

On Monday evening, Bill Adams was transferred to Stanford Hospital in the San Francisco Bay Area. He was listed in good condition after receiving spinal circulation injections and massage, but amputation of his feet was still likely. Surgery was scheduled for the following morning. Bill Adams had also begun to develop pneumonia. The following morning, however, surgery was canceled because circulation had begun to return to his feet. It was expected that Bill Adams might still lose his toes.

A week later, the Butte County Board of Supervisors requested an accounting of the Bill Adams rescue. Apparently, they were considering billing Bill Adams' county of residence for the cost associated with the rescue, but the undersheriff reported an expense of only $150. He told the Board of Supervisors that his team spent $90 in gasoline and only paid for 25 sandwiches and five gallons of coffee. Manpower was free. Bill Adams' brother, Thomas, told reporters in Oroville that he worked with a lot of search and rescue teams but, he said, "I have never seen it run better than it is here."

For news photos, Jack was dressed in a suit and tie, and Lt. Michelson wore his uniform; they were asked to stand near Bill Adams, as he lay in his hospital bed. Jack was uncomfortable with the photo session because it felt staged, and because it didn't represent the entire group responsible for the man's rescue. The next day, Jack was happy to see he was not in the newspaper. The picture displayed in the local news was of Bill's mother standing over him in his hospital bed with a smile on her face. Lt. Michelson was pictured standing next to her.

In addition to giving equal credit where it was due, Jack was also the type of teammate to recognize his own limitations and call for help from those with qualities he lacked or training he hadn't received, whenever needed. An example of this occurred one month after the rescue of Bill Adams when Jack and fellow members of the Butte County Search and Rescue Team were called back to the area around Feather Falls.

On Thursday, March 25, 1976, a nineteen-year-old airman stationed at Beale Air Force Base, forty miles south of Oroville, hiked with some of his friends to the lookout of Feather Falls, one of the nation's tallest waterfalls, with some friends. At 4:30 P.M., the airman and another man climbed around a barricade for a better look at the bottom of the falls nearly 600 feet below. As the men made their way back to the lookout, the airman was heard saying, "Oh my God!" The other man turned back and saw the airman falling hundreds of feet to the ground below.

The airman's friends hiked out of the falls and contacted authorities; later that evening they met with Sgt. Jack Smith of the Butte County Sheriff's Office Search and Rescue Team. It wasn't the first time the search and rescue team had been called to the area (and it wouldn't be the last), so Jack consulted with other members of his team and assessed the situation. Because of the difficulty in reaching the location of the airman, the likelihood that the airman was deceased, and because it was late in the day, they decided it was safest to wait until the following morning to retrieve the airman's body. The Search and Rescue Coordinator, Lt. Ken Mickelson, told local media, "There are several places in there where our own guys could get killed in the dark. If there had been any possibility that he was alive, they would have gone in..."

The following morning, Friday, Jack led a team of ten people, four of whom were experienced climbers, on what was expected to be a six-to-seven-hour recovery mission to the airman's body resting 560 feet below the lookout. Jack anticipated his team would bring the body out with a rope and a stretcher. Unfortunately, the team was unable to reach the airman's body because of the danger in navigating around and through the sheer granite cliffs. A free-rappel of 560 feet from the lookout was possible, but dangerous even for the most professional of climbers—and by the end of the day the climbers were exhausted from their efforts and suffering leg cramps.

Jack and his team, including the local climbers, gave the recovery a second attempt on Saturday, but once again, they were unsuccessful. Other options, including a risky free-rappel of 1800 feet from a helicopter in the gusty winds of a canyon, were considered, but Jack and his team opted for a safer option—turn the recovery mission over to a group of people with more experience. The next day, Sunday, seven professional rock climbers from the San Francisco Bay Area were flown to Oroville to assist in the recovery effort.

At 11:30 A.M., one rock climber rappelled nearly 600 feet on a nylon rope from the Feather Falls Lookout. He had trouble keeping his footing due to the spray from the falls making everything slippery. A second rope was lowered with a portable gurney attached. Two other men climbed part-way down to assist with the ropes. When the rock climber reached the airman, there, on the same ledge as his body, were signs which read, "Dangerous Area; Do Not Go Beyond The Rails." Apparently, the signs had been removed from the area of the lookout above and thrown over by vandals.

Several hours later, the volunteer team from the San Francisco Bay Area, with the help of Jack and other members of the Butte County Search and Rescue Team hand-hauling the body and the gurney up the steep cliffs, the airmen's body was retrieved. On Sunday, his remains were sent to a local mortuary and then back to Beale Air Force Base. A coroner confirmed that the airman died upon impact.

Little Jackie Smith Became...

CHAPTER SEVEN
A Man of Principle

By all accounts, after eleven years as a deputy, Jack was at the top of his game. He made a career out of helping people, he loved it, and he did it exceptionally well. Jack had also continued inching his way toward a bachelor's degree, earning and surpassing an Associate of Arts Degree in Police Science, and part of that education included a Women in Law Enforcement class. Jack knew that women entering a predominately male-dominated field were in some ways facing an uphill battle, and he wanted to learn how he could better support the growing number of female colleagues he was working with in the various law enforcement agencies. Jack also obtained a Community College Teaching Credential and was one of several officers chosen to teach Police Science classes at Butte Community College.

What few people knew in the mid-1970s, however, was that Jack began to suffer from symptoms of anxiety. It started with his chest tightening, and he had trouble breathing. Jack's anxiety intensified to a point that he was also blacking out. One day, Jack was riding in the passenger's seat of a patrol car with one of his fellow deputies when he felt as if he was losing touch with reality; he held onto the dashboard to make sure he could continue to identify something real until the feeling subsided.

Jack was a physically fit man in his mid-thirties, so heart issues were unlikely. He had smoked cigarettes since his teen-age years, though, so had his heart checked out anyway. Heart problems were ruled out. Jack worried that whatever he was going through might be the same problem his mother, Victoria, had before she died. Victoria was in her early thirties when Smitty appeared after an eight-year absence. They reunited, and within a year, her emotional state became more and more unstable. Victoria appeared to suffer from depression and anxiety, and she experienced periods of aggression and hostility, all of which were out of character for her. Jack wondered if he should see a counselor for his anxiety. Then, one night when Jack was arresting a crime suspect, the man spit in his face. Jack had his flashlight in his hand at the time and responded by striking the man in the head with it. Jack never acted or re-acted in a violent manner with anyone, and at that point, he was convinced he needed help, so he sought counseling.

Work seemed to be the place where Jack experienced the worst of his symptoms, so a reflection back to the mid-1960s on some of the most difficult situations he faced at work may have helped to shed some light on an underlying source of his troubles. The first incident of distress occurred when Jack was a rookie patrolman riding in the passenger seat of the patrol car when a call came in to assist a single-car accident on Highway 70. Jack and his partner arrived on scene to find a car engulfed in flames. They could hear people screaming inside, but the heat from the fire was too intense for them to get into the car. Four bodies were recovered and later identified as teenagers. Jack talked to his wife, Ann, for quite some time about how difficult it was to get the image and the screaming sounds out of his mind.

Naturally, considering the nature of the work, there were other incidents of disturbing injury, death, and unsolved cases. As Jack ascended the ranks in the Sheriff's Department, he was never one to sit behind a desk delegating responsibilities to others—Jack was on the front line, so there were many stories he could share with a counselor. And he was so dedicated to his cases, he had a hard time leaving them at work. Jack was known to leave his house and search for evidence in a case during his time off. It wasn't, however, easy to know if any particular event had had a long-term impact on Jack because he had a tendency to tell stories which ended with statements like, "but that's part of the job" or "but children have a way of adapting" as a way of minimizing how deeply it may have affected him.

One work-related issue that Jack was having a difficult time coping in the mid-1970s revolved around criminal behavior among some of his fellow law enforcement officers. As a person, Jack held himself at a high standard of moral character—not just in his personal life, but in every aspect of his life. He knew that people may not always behave at their best, but when it came to people who chose to serve the public, Jack had higher expectations. He also believed that when people made mistakes, they needed to own up to them.

Some of the activities Jack was aware of at the time and were weighing heavily on his mind included a colleague in the Sheriff's Department who was arrested for burglarizing homes. Jack couldn't wrap his head around it. There were also rumors that a couple of law enforcement officers assaulted a woman at a party in Oroville and that it may have been brushed under the rug. The officers may not have worked in the same agency as Jack, but he was disturbed, and, to him, the thought of anyone abusing their position in law enforcement to commit a crime and then cover it up was simply inconceivable.

Details of Jack's life outside of work also came out in counseling. Jack and Ann separated when Vickie was three years old and Alan was turning five. They divorced by the following year. Ann kept primary custody of Alan and Vickie, but Jack had an open invitation anytime he wanted to see them. Then, in 1975, Ann moved Alan and Vickie to Sacramento. This was difficult for Jack because his accessibility to them changed, and he was no longer able to physically contribute to their caretaking as often as he had. Jack also felt it was much more difficult for him to help keep them safe. So, Jack did what he could; he frequently drove to Sacramento and took his children on dates, just as he had when they lived in Oroville, and Ann drove the kids back to Oroville periodically to visit her family and to spend time with their dad.

Two years after Jack's divorce from Ann, he married Patricia. She had a daughter, Lori, from a previous marriage who was a few years older than Alan and Vickie, so Jack took on the role of stepfather. Patricia was active in church, and because Jack was a man of Christian faith, he easily reengaged in attending Sunday church services. Jack, Patricia and Lori were also horse enthusiasts, so they spent a lot of time riding and caring for their horses. Jack's marriage to

Jack with his second wife, Patricia, and one of their horses.

Jack horseback riding with his stepdaughter, Lori, during a camping trip near the Feather River Canyon.

Patricia ended after a year and a half, though it was amicable, and they remained friends.

After two divorces, Jack adjusted back into life as a single man. He dated occasionally but nothing too serious—and it certainly wasn't because the opportunity didn't present itself. Unmarried, Jack was one of the most handsome and eligible gentlemen in town, and there was never a shortage of women attempting to gain his attention. But Jack was sociable enough that he was never lonely, and he enjoyed his single life—particularly the solitude and simple living that came with it.

A deeper look into Jack's family led to an exchange with his counselor about his parents, but those discussions were relatively short. At the time of Jack's anxiety attacks, Smitty was living in New Zealand with his wife, Edna. The only other family members Jack had as a local support system were his dad's aging siblings and their spouses—Uncle George and his wife, Aunt Avis, who lived on the outskirts of Oroville, and Aunt Gracie and her husband, Wilber, who lived in Sacramento. Most of Jack's interactions with his aunts and uncles happened because Jack visited their homes to check on their well-being. Jack also maintained relationships with his former in-laws, both Ann's and Patricia's extended families. Jack received repeated invitations to attend family functions from them, most often he thanked them and respectfully declined, unless Lori, Alan, and/or Vickie would be there, then he would attend if he could.

When counseling sessions took Jack back into time with his mother and his childhood, there was even less to talk about—most memories led to more questions than answers. Jack's father left when he was an infant, and Jack didn't know why. Jack's mother had been unable to care for him on her own, so he spent weekends with her and weekdays in a foster home. Sometimes Jack's weekends with his mother were spent at a family function at her parents' home. Jack didn't know why he had to live in a foster home when his mother's parents and siblings were nearby. However, Jack considered it a happy childhood because he was surrounded by loving people and lots of kids to play with.

Jack's dad reappeared, and his parents reunited when he was eight years old; Jack said that's when everything changed. Jack's mother began having mental problems and she was placed in a hospital, but, at the time, Jack didn't really understand what was happening to his mother. Then, at the age of ten, Jack was living with his dad when his mother died, and all he was told was that she committed suicide by jumping from a building top. After his mother's death, Jack was shuffled between foster homes and his dad's home, mostly throughout California but also in Alaska, until his junior year at Oroville High School when he was able to live on his own. Jack believed he adapted relatively well to the challenges in his childhood and into his formation as an adult.

In between counseling sessions, Jack was still committed to conducting his job the only way he knew how — to the same high standard he had always applied himself. In early April 1976, a man was flying his single-engine Cessna 182 from Twin Falls, Idaho, back to his home in Chico. At 8 P.M., the pilot contacted the Redding flight station indicating he was unsure of his location but believed he was somewhere near

Jack on horseback

Jack on his motorcycle

Jack fishing

Jack with his step-daughter, Lori's, cat during a family hike to the top of Table Mountain

the mountain town of Quincy. Two men from the Oroville area were camping in the mountains that evening, and they saw the lights of a plane flying at about 2500 feet inside a canyon area surrounded by mountains as high as 5000 feet. The plane looped out of the canyon but then returned, and the two men watched as the plane slammed into the mountain-side and burst into flames about a mile from Feather Falls (the same region of the county in which the two men and the dog had been lost in the snow and where the airmen fell to his death.)

From their campsite, the two men were able to climb to the scene of the crash and put out a small brush fire. When the flames died down, the two men saw the remains of the pilot. The men knew it was not safe to hike out of the wilderness at night, so the next morning, one man stayed to watch the wreckage in case another fire was to erupt, while the other man made his way to a nearby town to notify authorities. At 9:30 A.M., a full call-out of the Butte County Search and Rescue was made.

Thirteen men, including Jack, responded to the call. Having hiked and camped in the mountainous regions outside of Oroville with friends during high school and after his return from Bible College and the Navy, and, at times, all alone whenever he felt the need for peaceful time away from work and personal life, Jack knew the area of the plane crash well. It wasn't accessible to four-wheel vehicles or mountain bikes, so Jack grabbed his horse and rode it into the wilderness. Jack borrowed a second horse from his ex-wife, Patricia, to pull behind him up the mountain as a way of transporting the pilot's remains from the crash scene. Another search and rescue team member rode his horse and two others rode trail bikes. The remains of a 43-year-old, male pilot were brought out of the mountains by 6:30 P.M.

Three days later, in a story titled, "Pilot Disorientation Blamed for Crash," the *Oroville Mercury* newspaper reported that Sgt. Jack Smith took an aircraft accident analyst from the Cessna Aircraft Corporation on horseback into the rugged wilderness and to the canyon wall where the plane crashed and burned several days earlier. The analyst's assessment, as Sgt. Smith later told reporters, determined the pilot crashed because he was disoriented, that he flew low to stay below the clouds and get a point of orientation, and when he noticed the mountains, he gave it full throttle and attempted to bank left, but was unable to avoid impact.

When Jack talked to people, be it a counselor or anyone else, he gladly shared stories he wanted to tell, but it was the stories he only gave a brief mention of, or those he accidently allowed to slip through, that may have had more meaning to him than he was letting on. Eventually, however, counseling brought to the surface a deeply hidden and important story. It occurred a few short years into Jack's career as an investigator — before the Helen Gould murder, before retrieving the Biggs youth from Idaho, before the rescue of Bill Adams from the snow-covered mountain and many others — but even at the time Jack was in counseling, he found it difficult to talk about.

Just before midnight on a Saturday night in the early 1970s, a five-month old boy was taken to the Oroville Hospital

Emergency Room by his parents. The parents told the doctors the baby had suffered two convulsions. A doctor examined the baby and found that he appeared to have lost his vision, his brain was swelling, and he had two bruises on his back. The child was admitted to the hospital, and x-rays were taken. Doctors found evidence of fractures on the left leg and left arm that appeared to be approximately one month old and were never treated. They also found a fracture to the skull and believed the child sustained it within ten days prior — possibly accounting for the recent convulsions. Early the next morning, the baby was transferred to a larger hospital in a nearby town.

Due to the child appearing dirty and undernourished and the extent of injuries, the doctors were concerned about potential child neglect and abuse. The mother was questioned by doctors. She told doctors the baby was born two months premature, weighed only 3 pounds 13 ounces at birth, and that he had to stay in the hospital for the first five weeks after birth. She believed the baby's injuries were a result of him having fallen off the bed twice and being dumped onto the floor when their young daughter knocked over his crib five to six weeks earlier. When the doctors told the mother about the fracture to the arm, she admitted that she noticed he hadn't been able to use his arm for a while. The mother attempted to explain the child's lack of nourishment as a result of him not having had an appetite for the previous ten days.

Hospital staff contacted the Sheriff's Department, and Jack began an investigation. When he arrived at the hospital, the doctor informed him there was a hemorrhage in the baby's brain and that bloody fluid was being drained to release the pressure against the skull. This appeared to have improved the baby's appetite and mobility since being admitted. The doctor believed brain surgery was likely.

From the pediatrician's opinion, the baby could have experienced a skull fracture if he had fallen from a three-foot distance and landed on his head on a hard surface. However, he had expressed it as improbable that a one-year old sibling pushed a crib over due to his experience with children crawling in and out of cribs without them dumping over. The doctor also stated that the baby likely would not have been able to roll or move off the bed unless assisted or put near the edge—particularly a baby born prematurely who only had the physical capabilities of a three-month old. Based on the condition of the baby, the pediatrician believed he only received a minimal amount of attention. The doctor did not believe the child should be returned to the parents; he was concerned the boy was living in a hostile and neglectful home.

The radiologist informed Jack that the bone structure appeared to be of normal development and free of disease and that in his opinion, the fractures on the leg and arm likely would have been from a sharp blow from being hit or falling, or from the limb being grabbed. As for the skull fracture, the doctor believed that it could have occurred from falling from a bed or a crib. The skull fracture was not the direct cause of injury, he added, but rather the tearing of the brain upon impact at the time of the injury.

Of the numerous unbending rules Jack followed in his personal and professional life was that children should never be harmed – preferably not by other children and certainly not by adults. Jack believed to his core that children should be protected, and one way of protecting a child who may have been abused was to believe the child until a proper investigation is conducted and, if needed, a fair and just trial proved otherwise. Jack may have adopted this belief from his experience with his own parents or other people, he may have learned it from the bible, maybe from law enforcement training or in his college class on parent-child relationships, but however it was planted, it was seeded deep. The baby Jack saw lying in a hospital bed couldn't speak for himself, but his injuries, both previous and current, spoke for him, and the injuries indicated he was likely neglected or abused, or both.

Five days after the baby was admitted to the hospital, Jack and his partner interviewed the parents at their home. Again, the parents said that the baby was born premature and that the hospital released him to them when his weight exceeded 5 pounds. The parents picked fruit for a living, so their children were placed in childcare facility while they worked. When the baby was a few months old, he fell off the bed. Around the same time, he was dumped over in a bassinet and stopped using his arm. The parents didn't take him to the doctor because it appeared to have gotten better. A month later, the baby began having convulsions. At that point, the parents took the baby to the hospital where the baby was observed and released.

The mother told Jack that a few weeks later she was changing the baby's diaper and when she left for a moment to discard the dirty diaper, the baby fell off the bed again. In the days to follow, the baby lost his appetite and started having more convulsions. Both parents denied abusing the child though the baby had been left in the care of other people; the parents also did not believe anyone else had abused him either.

Jack and his partner inspected the home and determined it was not clean, but the older child appeared in good health. When Jack asked to see the crib in which the baby slept and was toppled over in, the mother would not allow him into the bedroom to see it. She brought a bassinet to him in the front room as though it was the bed in which the baby was dumped over in. In addition, the mother would not allow Jack to see the bed from which the baby fell during a diaper change — but she described it to him.

When contacting the welfare department, Jack was told the parents had attempted to apply for medical insurance a month earlier but were denied, and that the baby's father became irate with social services staff and had to be escorted off the premises. Jack's partner later contacted Child Protective Services and asked them to investigate the parents' home and determine the safety of the older child.

When Jack was married to Ann, in addition to their own children, Alan and Vickie, they also temporarily took in foster children — another way Jack wanted to give back to the community. During the investigation of the hospitalized baby, Jack was married to Patricia, and they began discussing the possibility of taking this baby into their home, possibly adopting him if the parents lost their rights. Jack wanted to give the baby a loving home.

No one knew why Jack felt such a connection to this child; maybe because the boy resembled Alan when he was a baby, or possibly Jack empathized with the baby because of the fear he likely experienced under his parents' care. During Jack's childhood, there were a few occasions he was fearful at home. After Smitty and Victoria reunited when Jack was eight years old, he feared there were times his dad would leave and never return—mostly because his dad's repeated absence seemed to cause the decline of his mother's mental state. At one point, after Smitty had been gone for several days, Jack was playing while his mother was cooking. She got upset at the noise he was making and started hitting him with a pan. When she realized what she was doing, she started crying and apologizing to him.

There were two other occasions after that where Jack feared his mother might harm him. Once, when Jack and his mom were walking together through a field, Victoria took his hand and guided him off the path to the edge of large crater in the ground. She talked about jumping in. Jack knew the hole was too deep for anyone to jump safely, so he pulled backwards, away from the edge of the pit. His mother, however, stood firm and refused to release his hand. A moment later, however, she seemed to come to her senses, and they went on their way.

A short time after that, when Jack and his parents were living in Sacramento near Smitty's brother, George, and his wife, Avis, Jack was outside walking his dog. He heard his mother calling his name, and just as he began to make his way back toward home, his Aunt Avis ran up to him and told him his mother was looking for him, but his mother had an ax in her hand. Avis told Jack to run to his elementary school and hide. So, Jack took his dog, ran to his school, and hid under a wooden walkway. When he returned home later, the police were arresting his mother. That was the day she was taken to the mental hospital. She died a few months later.

Eleven days after the baby was admitted to the hospital, Jack was notified that the child's condition worsened, and he was placed on life support. Jack immediately contacted the doctor and asked if additional x-rays could be done. The doctor told him they could not do x-rays on the baby in his current condition. Jack asked if surgery was an option, but again, he was told it could not be done at that time. The doctor said the baby may not survive. Jack requested to be contacted if there was any change.

Child Protective Services was asked if an investigation had been done of the home and the older child. It had not, but Jack was assured it would happen. If it was determined that the older child would be removed from the home, Jack requested that x-rays be done on that child as well. Two days later, just before dawn, Jack received a call informing him that the baby died. Jack immediately contacted his partner who then got approval for an autopsy. It was completed later that afternoon.

With the boy's passing, Jack was determined to find out if the parents or anyone else contributed to the injuries and subsequent death of the child. He was told that the parents had visited a funeral home and two days later the burial occurred, so immediately after the funeral, Jack's partner contacted the baby's father and asked him to come to the sheriff's office. He complied. There, Jack talked to the father about the suspicious nature of the child's injuries and death. Jack suggested the father and the mother should take a polygraph since they were the primary caretakers of the child. The father became angry, denied ever mistreating his child and stated that he didn't trust polygraphs. The father claimed he didn't spend much time with the child, didn't develop much love for him, and that his marriage was falling apart, and he was probably going to be leaving his wife. The mother arrived a short time later and agreed to a polygraph to be scheduled the following day. Relatives who lived in the home and cared for the baby also agreed to a polygraph.

Jack believed the parents or someone in contact with the baby were involved in the child's injuries and subsequent death, severe neglect at the very least, but in the end, there was no conviction for child neglect, child abuse, or for the death of the baby. Jack was extremely disappointed with the outcome, and he worried about the safety of the other child in the home. He wasn't sure if someone outsmarted the system and got away with murder, if the limitations of social services and the legal system failed the child, or worse, if *he* himself fell short in his investigative work, but whatever happened, Jack could not rest easy with the outcome. To make matters worse, Jack believed the cause of death as described by the family was misleading, if not an outright lie—the child's death was reported as a result of his preterm birth.

While continuing counseling, Jack also carried on with work. After assisting in the recovery of the plane crash victim,

Jack successfully completed a months-long sting operation in which nine people were arrested for home burglaries resulting in $10k-$15k dollars in stolen items—and crimes in which adults used children aged 5-15 years old as the burglars. He also worked with a neighboring county in a lengthy narcotic sales investigation.

Before the end of the year, whether it was anxiety from having experienced childhood trauma (later known as PTSD) and something he probably assumed was resolved, or stress from his job and/or his personal life, or inherited mental illness, Jack's mental state had not returned to what he considered healthy—and he still felt guilty about the flashlight incident when the man spit in his face. Whatever it was, though, Jack realized he was not doing himself, his family, his friends, his colleagues, or the community any good by continuing to work as a deputy. He felt it was time for a different line of work, so much to the dismay of a lot of people, Jack submitted his intent to retire from the Butte County Sheriff's Department.

Leaving law enforcement was not an easy decision for Jack. He knew he was leaving a career for which he seemed to have been born, and that finding the types of relationships he had established in the sheriff's department would be difficult in another profession. Jack knew there were colleagues he could trust with his life, and that wasn't easy to come by. Some colleagues had become very good friends to Jack and he to them. One night, Jack had just finished his shift when, as he often did, he joined the dispatchers, Mary Jane and Sally, for some small talk while completing his paperwork. He found his colleague and friend, Mary Jane, crying. She was upset over news that an ex-boyfriend had gotten married, so Jack suggested she go home, and he finished her shift for her. Another friend and colleague of Jack's was told by the undersheriff in 1969 to show up for work even though the man's wife was in labor. Jack heard about his friend's wife, and that she was alone in labor at the hospital, so he made a surprise visit. Fathers weren't allowed in the labor room when Alan and Vickie were born in 1965 and 1967, but that rule had changed by 1969, and though Jack didn't have experience with labor support, he went into the woman's labor room to see if he could help. Once there, Jack couldn't think of anything to do but squeeze the laboring woman's toe to distract her from the pain of each contraction. When she was taken to a delivery room, Jack waited at the hospital until the birth was announced, then Jack called his friend at the Sheriff's Department to inform him he had a healthy baby girl.

There were sad days within the sheriff's department in the weeks leading up to Gentleman Jack's retirement, but Jack felt to his core that it was the right thing to do. He also knew, despite some the corrupt outliers (who also should have found a different line of work), that he was leaving the department in the hands of a lot people who were as dedicated to professionalism in service as he was. There were a lot of good men and women in the various departments of law enforcement in and around Butte County, and Jack was honored to have worked alongside them.

Before Jack's retirement date arrived, two men escaped

Jack at work near the end of his career as a detective

from the Butte County Jail in Oroville. The men were reported to have stolen a car and were driving northbound on Highway 70, so an all-points bulletin was issued. When Dispatcher Mary Jane Perrucci received a radio call from Jack, he was in pursuit of the escapees. A short time later, other law enforcement personnel joined him.

With lights on and siren blaring, officers followed the jail escapees up Highway 70 into the Feather River Canyon—

passing waterfalls, steep cliffs, and wildlife—while dispatcher Mary Jane Perrucci remained in radio contact with them. Mary Jane received updates on changing locations of the suspects while she followed along on a map and provided the officers with various routes to position themselves to block the escapees' route.

Well into the winding canyon roads, the fleeing men turned off the highway and onto a mountain road. Mary Jane's map showed no other option but for the officers to continue following directly behind the escapees. Jack, however, knew the area so well, he turned, by himself, onto a different mountain road. It wasn't on Mary Jane's map, so she could no longer give him directions, but Jack knew where he was, and he ended stopping the escapees' car from one direction while the other law enforcement pinned them in from other directions. The men were captured and returned to the Butte County Jail. Jack got his wish to Code 3 through the Feather River Canyon—and Deputy Butch Ellis got his wish, too, because he wasn't a passenger in Jack's car when it happened.

Little Jackie Smith Became...

CHAPTER EIGHT
Patient and Faithful

In the years following Victoria's death, Jack was reminded of his mother each time the song *Blue Moon* resurfaced. In the 1950s, the song was revived through recordings by popular musicians like Billie Holiday, Elvis, Ella Fitzgerald, and Glenn Miller and his orchestra. The song was also featured in movies released nearly every year in the decade of the fifties, in fact, in 1957 alone (the year Jack graduated from high school), it could be heard in three separate movies.

The 1950s recordings of *Blue Moon* were successful, but it was the Marcel's doo-wop version, released in 1961 when Jack was in the military, that proved the song was still relevant more than fifteen years after it first was written. It also proved the song could cross genres and still top the charts. Despite the success of the doo-wop version, however, there was still a preference among many for the song at its ballad roots, as heard recorded and released several times in the sixties by artists like Sam Cooke, Frank Sinatra, Dean Martin, and in 1967, the year Vickie was born, The Supremes.

From the late 1960s to the late 1970s, Jack was so busy with life in law enforcement and reminders of the challenges he faced in childhood, he didn't realize he hadn't been exposed to certain loving memories and good times with his mother. Of course, Jack had his daughter who shared his mother's name, and she was a constant reminder of the wonderful woman his mother had been, but that changed in the summer of 1978 when another reminder resurfaced. A year and a half after Jack's retirement from the Butte County Sheriff's Department, the movie *Grease* appeared in theatres. The musical portrayed experiences of teenagers in the late 1950s, the same time frame Jack was in high school. Nearing the age of forty in the late seventies, Jack wasn't as much of a moviegoer; neither did he frequent the indoor Oroville State Theatre as often as he had when he was younger, but a drive-in theater was located near the main strip, so there was no way anyone driving through town in the evenings could avoid catching the sights and sounds of clips of the biggest blockbuster of the summer. Passing by the movie screen during the dance scene that played the song "Blue Moon," reminded Jack of a certain nostalgia that came with the song his mother loved so much.

Also, in 1978, Jack was still in the transition phase from a career in law enforcement to the next career choice. Jack had been working at the largest motel in Oroville, Prospector's Village, but he didn't plan to stay there; Jack had something else in mind. During the 1970s, he had met several people in Oroville who picked up quite lucrative seasonal work, so he was considering that. It would require a substantial financial investment and he would have to leave Oroville, but not for long periods of time, and he wouldn't have to go far.

Each year in the decade of the 1970s, mostly between the months of April through September, large numbers of people spilled over the California coastal mountains into the Northern California coastal town of Ft. Bragg—one of the West Coast's largest salmon fishing ports. Tommy Ancona, a former fisherman, owned a marine supply store in Ft. Bragg. Ancona answered the newcomers' questions about fishing, he drew diagrams for them, and he sold them supplies they needed. Several years later he said, "I built my business on them. It was like the Gold Rush era, and I sold pots and pans to the gold miners."

Ancona said the newcomers came from all walks of life and from all over. Some were retired and/or lured by the romance of living on the water and the coastal life, wanting to get away from the heat of the Central Valley or away from another life, while others were just people looking for a new way to make money. Ancona said, "There were hundreds and hundreds of them. It was like they came out of the trees.

"Salmon fishing was the easiest for someone who had never fished before, and it required the least amount of money to invest. A lot of them had experience in sport fishing and when they found out how lucrative salmon fishing could be, they said, 'Hey I can do this and make money at it.' And think about it, how many sports can turn into someone's commercial business? It was a madhouse, but everyone made money."

There was, however, a high turnover of fisherman when the reality of the fishing industry didn't live up to some of the expectations. The money was there, but it was cold, often foggy, and it was a lot of hard work. Ancona said, "The people who came had to be brave. It's impressive for people to leave their comfort zones. They could have just stayed where they were comfortable."

So, after much consideration, Jack cashed out his retirement and bought a fishing boat named the *Ramona R.* In spring 1979, he placed his Samsonite luggage and the rest of his personal belongings into a storage unit in Oroville, drove west across the valley and over the coastal mountains, and became one of the newcomers to Ft. Bragg.

Jack liked the simple living environment of a small bedroom, bathroom and kitchenette — the *Ramona R.* offered him that. Jack was at a point in his life that he wanted a certain degree of solitude — life on the sea offered him that. Jack hoped for a healthy paycheck — the salmon gave him that; in fact, his income as a fisherman increased so far beyond what he expected, while he was fishing, Jack sent Ann double (or even more) of the monthly amount he was required to pay for child support.

Unfortunately, on May 21, 1979, things changed. The day began without incident; the sun rose over the mountains into clear skies and the sea was calm. Jack went out fishing and stayed on the sea through most of the day. Then, at 3:47 P.M., the U.S. Coast Guard received an impact distress call on channel 16. A man's voice radioed that he had hit the rocks just off the jetty of the Noyo River inlet and he was taking on water. The Coast Guard vessel, *Point Ledge*, arrived on scene at 3:54 P.M. and began pumping water off the boat. Thirty minutes later, still assisted by the Coast Guard, the man's boat hit a rock again and began to take on more water. A relative of Jack's second wife, Patricia, lived in the area and just happened to be driving across a bridge near the scene of the accident. She recognized the sinking boat in the water. "Oh God!," she said, "It's Jack!"

The Ramona R.

She was right. The Coast Guard referred to Jack as the captain of the boat, and a local news reporter caught a picture of Jack standing on the deck of the *Ramona R.*, as it was partially underwater; the Coast Guard Cutter was nearby. The Mendocino Beacon placed the photo on its front page.

Jack was in the news again, but this time he wasn't referred to as a graduating high school senior, the father of a newborn daughter, a deputy with the Butte County Sheriff's Department, or the victim of a convenience store robbery, he was

Noyo River inlet, Fort Bragg, Calif. (photo courtesy of Trista Wilson)

identified in the local Ft. Bragg newspaper as the boat's owner, Jack Smith of Oroville. The caption in the newspaper read:

> Jack Smith of Oroville, owner of the 38-foot vessel *Romona R.*, was rescued Monday by Coast Guardsmen aboard the Point Ledge. Although Smith was uninjured, his boat remained half-sunk as late as Wednesday. The Point Ledge was at the scene of the accident for several hours attempting to save the boat, however their pumping efforts failed, and the boat went under. Smith reportedly was bringing in

his fish lines at the mouth of the harbor when
he lost control of the vessel and crashed off the
rocks. The boat is valued at more than $25,000.

Jack was safe, but he lost nearly everything of monetary
value when his boat sank. After paying to have the boat
pulled from the water and sent to a boat wrecking yard, Jack
returned to Oroville with only $4 to his name. To some
degree, Jack's pride also took a hit; even though the incident
was considered a freak accident, Jack still wondered if there
was something he could have done differently. After
returning to Oroville, Jack placed a copy of the newspaper
article into his Samsonite and had no intention of looking
back at that memory for quite some time.

In the three years that followed the sinking of the *Ramona
R.*, Jack experienced one of the worst personal and financial
setbacks of his adult life. He worked odd jobs, but nothing
seemed to last or be a good fit. Jack lived paycheck to
paycheck, or at times, no paycheck at all. At times, he had to
borrow money from his friends.

Adding to Jack's troubles was news that his dad, Smitty,
was diagnosed with cancer. Jack had come to accept that
Smitty wasn't really fit to father a young child, but he believed
his dad loved him. Jack fondly remembered being a young
adult and bonding with Smitty. The two took a road trip to
Oatman, Arizona, where Smitty pointed out where he
worked, and where they lived at the time of Jack's birth.
When Jack visited Smitty in Missouri after leaving San Jose
Bible College, but before enlisting in the Navy, Smitty owned

a brand-new convertible Ford, and on several occasions, he allowed Jack to drive his cousins and their friends in it to Rockaway Beach at the Lake of the Ozarks. During Jack's four years in the Navy, whenever he took temporary leave time, he indicated he could be reached by mail at Smitty's home in Carmichael, just outside the city limits of Sacramento, California.

Jack appreciated that Smitty turned out to be a good grandfather. Though Smitty moved to New Zealand when Jack's children were young, whenever Smitty and his New Zealand-native wife, Edna, visited Oroville, they showered Alan and Vickie with gifts, money, and a lot of loving attention.

Smitty opted for cancer treatment in the United States, specifically in Sacramento so he could spend time with his family. During his treatment sessions, Smitty stayed at a hotel in downtown Sacramento; Jack drove from Oroville and picked Alan and Vickie up from their home (also in Sacramento), and they would all go to lunch with Smitty and then visit him for a while at his hotel. Jack always kept his financial status relatively private, so Smitty was not aware that his son often borrowed money for these visits to take place.

Smitty lost his battle with cancer in April 1982. It added to the difficult time Jack was having, but he didn't let people see him down and out, and nothing dimmed that beautiful smile regardless of his personal troubles. Jack honored Smitty in his final years by making sure his father was surrounded by family, despite the financial cost and time away from search-

Smitty with photos of his grandchildren, Alan and Vickie (late 1960s)

Jack with his father, Smitty, and stepmother, Edna (1970s)

ing for his next job, because through it all, Jack had faith that everything was going to be okay. Jack's second wife, Patricia, later said, "Jack had the patience of Job."

In October 1982, the hard times appeared to be passing when Jack returned to law enforcement—this time without the likelihood of being exposed to abused and neglected children—but he would have to leave California. Jack accepted an offer for a security job at an Army base in Tooele, Utah, a small town on the outskirts of Salt Lake City. Jack's former brother-in-law, Sonny (one of Ann's younger brothers), lived in Tooele with his wife, Helen, and their four sons. Upon Sonny's insistence, Jack moved in with Sonny and his family until he got his own place.

Jack's responsibilities as a security guard at the Army Depot included dispatch, checkpoint, and area patrol. He monitored close circuit television and computerized fire detection systems. He patrolled camp and operating area facilities, responded to fire and medical emergencies, monitored access into facilities, conducted searches of vehicles and people, x-rayed parcels and personal effects. He participated in exercises involving sabotage and espionage attempts, hostage situation, bomb threats, riots, and crowd control. Jack's duties also included the shift schedule, timecards, payroll, and the training of 16-20 officers.

Two months after Jack began his work at the Tooele Army Depot, he was awarded a Certificate of Achievement in recognition of numerous exceptional abilities, and it was obvious he had returned to law enforcement with the same amount of skill and efficiency as when he left it in 1976. One month later, Jack accepted an offer for a better paying security job at the Chevron Construction Camp in Casper, Wyoming. A few months after that, Jack was offered an even higher wage security job—one that would require him to move even further away from his family and friends in Northern California. After much contemplation, Jack accepted the job offer, and in May 1983, he began work at an ARCO oil drilling site at Prudhoe Bay, Alaska—located where the northern coast of Alaska meets the Arctic Ocean.

Living relatively close to the north pole, Jack learned to adapt to months of prolonged sunlight, then prolonged sunset and extreme weather conditions that sometimes dropped to minus 100 degrees; all the while he was maintaining safety on the oil fields. But Jack adjusted well. He enjoyed spending time with his co-workers in the employer-provided communal living accommodations, exercise facilities, entertainment options, and the cafeteria-style food. Time at the top of the world provided Jack the simple, routine life he enjoyed, an income higher than wages he earned as deputy sheriff, and time alone when he wanted it.

At the time, Alan and Vickie were in their teen years, and Jack made sure they always had a way to reach him by phone; even if he was in a security checkpoint shack during a blizzard, they knew they could call. Jack decided, however, the best way to maintain regular contact with his loved ones in California was by mail, so he made certain to send letters and cards to Alan, Vickie, and his other family and friends on birthdays and holidays. Also, every two or three months, Jack returned to California to visit family and friends for a week

AIR MILEAGE
FROM PRUDHOE
TO

NORTH POLE 1363
SOUTH POLE 11,087
MEXICO CITY 4041
DALLAS 3198   ANCHORAGE 640
NEW YORK 3233   VALDEZ 640
HONOLULU 3396   FAIRBANKS 398
LONDON 3872   JUNEAU 889
MOSCOW 3724   TOKYO 3487

Air miles from Prudhoe Bay, Alaska

or two.

Surrounded by nature, Jack enjoyed the beauty of Alaska. He showed Alan and Vickie images of wildlife that wandered onto the oil fields—a picture of a red fox burrowed into the snow or another inspecting a handrail for food, an Alaskan brown bear strolling across the barren land, a traveling herd of caribou, a long-tailed jaeger in flight, a beautiful Arctic fox seated regally on a snow bank, and four Arctic wolf pups in a small field of grass and flowers. At times, some of the wildlife came too close for comfort, as seen in Jack's picture of a caribou pecking around the corner of a shed, a polar bear on a mission running toward the person taking the photo, and another polar bear attempting to make its way through an occupied security shack window. Jack also showed Alan and Vickie pictures of snow-covered Alaskan peaks he took from his airplane window. Jack was, however, most impressed with the Aurora Borealis, or Northern Lights. He showed pictures and talked about how amazing it was to watch them.

Also in Alaska, Jack enjoyed observing the native Alaskans in their element. He had on VHS tape, or what he called "video film," footage of a whaling crew from an Inupiat Eskimo village in Nuiqsut, after they killed a 50-foot Bowhead whale and towed it near the shore where Jack worked. The hours-long video documented the butchering of the whale, which began in daylight showing a whale carcass upside down at the shoreline of the Arctic Sea. The video recording went on for hours of footage showing fat being stripped from the whale. By the next morning, all that remained of the whale was scraps strewn over a thin layer of snow on a dirt and gravel ground.

The following day, the *Anchorage Daily* newspaper reported the story of the whale dismemberment and informed readers that the whale carcass had been sent to a museum in Fairbanks. The newspaper also displayed pictures of the polar bears that caught the smell of the dead whale and ventured into Prudhoe Bay for the whale meat. The reporter indicated that up to seven polar bears feasted on scraps in the oil fields for 10 days, including the mother and two cubs that were visible on Jack's video. It was an exceptional news story because, although polar bears were known to pass through the Prudhoe Oil fields, they rarely hung out for long periods.

In August 1987, Congress contemplated opening Arctic National Wildlife Refuge (ANWR) to oil development, so members from the House Interior and Insular Affairs Committee, the House Merchant Marine and Fisheries

Jack in uniform at Prudhoe Bay

Committee, and the Senate Energy and National Resources Committee spent more than a week touring relevant sites in Alaska. The decision to drill for oil in the ANWR was controversial, so the visit was largely covered by daily news in the cities of Sitka, Fairbanks, Juneau, and Anchorage.

Jack volunteered to work overtime to drive a tour bus for members of Congress visiting Prudhoe Bay. One of the tours was mentioned in the news as having been one of the more adventurous experiences for the dignitaries. After one senator mentioned hoping to have seen more animals during their visit, disappointed at having only seen six musk oxen during a flight over the refuge, they saw fox, caribou and geese during their tour of Prudhoe Bay — at one point, the road the members of the Senate were on was blocked by a herd of caribou. Senator Frank Murkowski was quoted as saying, "That alone was worth the trip because that myth of the caribou not crossing the road was dispelled immediately."

The following month, Jack received the following letter from William E. Wade, Jr., President of ARCO Alaska, Inc.:

Dear Jack:

A note of thanks for your assistance during the recent '87 Congressional visits to our North Slope facilities.

These recent tours by the delegates were an important step in furthering our efforts to open the Coastal Plain of the Arctic National Wildlife

Refuge ("ANWR") to exploration and development. It is important Congress recognize the extraordinary potential of ANWR.

I appreciated you working over your normal
schedule driving the bus for us. Your courteous
and dependable manner added to the teamwork Wackenhut Security gave ARCO in helping make these special visits successful. Thank
you.

Two years later, in the fall of 1989, Jack returned to Oroville
and notified his family that he resigned from his job in Alaska.
His reason: several months earlier, in the spring of 1989 (a
year and a half after he drove members of Congress around
while they contemplated expanding the Alaskan oil fields),
disaster struck. From that point and throughout the summer
of 1989, Jack witnessed devastation of Alaskan wildlife and
natural beauty on an unprecedented scale.

Beginning in the 1970s, when Jack was still a deputy in
Northern California, jobs became plentiful in Alaska. Oil had
been discovered in the late sixties, a pipeline was built, then
oil was pumped from the ground at Prudhoe Bay and carried
through 800 miles of pipe to the port town of Valdez on the
southern end of Alaska. There, the oil was placed on ships and
transported to the lower 48 states. The process seemed to be a
successful one when Jack was hired to work as a security
guard on the Prudhoe Bay oil fields in 1983. However, that
changed on March 24, 1989, when one of the ships carrying

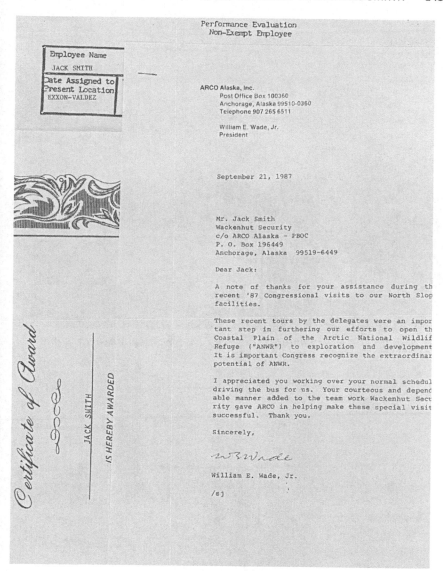

Performance Evaluation
Non-Exempt Employee

Employee Name
JACK SMITH

Date Assigned to
Present Location
EXXON-VALDEZ

ARCO Alaska, Inc.
Post Office Box 100360
Anchorage, Alaska 99510-0360
Telephone 907 265 6511

William E. Wade, Jr.
President

September 21, 1987

Mr. Jack Smith
Wackenhut Security
c/o ARCO Alaska - PBOC
P. O. Box 196449
Anchorage, Alaska 99519-6449

Dear Jack:

A note of thanks for your assistance during th
recent '87 Congressional visits to our North Slop
facilities.

These recent tours by the delegates were an impor
tant step in furthering our efforts to open th
Coastal Plain of the Arctic National Wildlif
Refuge ("ANWR") to exploration and development
It is important Congress recognize the extraordinar
potential of ANWR.

I appreciated you working over your normal schedul
driving the bus for us. Your courteous and depend
able manner added to the team work Wackenhut Secu
rity gave ARCO in helping make these special visit
successful. Thank you.

Sincerely,

William E. Wade, Jr.

/sj

Certificate of Award

JACK SMITH

IS HEREBY AWARDED

oil, the *Exxon Valdez,* went aground on a reef in Prince
William Sound as it was leaving the port. The impact
ruptured eight of the ship's 13 compartments and 250
thousand barrels of crude oil was spilled into the water. In

Jack's photo of Alaska mountains as seen from his seat on an airplane

Airport, Deadhorse and Prudhoe Bay, Alaska

response, Exxon and other oil companies went into emergency damage control. They scrambled to assemble more than 10,000 contract employees for oil-spill duty. Base Camp was set up in the town of Valdez, and Jack was one of the people sent by his employer from the northern slope of Alaska to the southern coastline clean-up zone.

Known by some as the Switzerland of Alaska, Valdez was a small town of approximately 3000 residents. It wasn't equipped for the numbers needed to accommodate the disaster, so Exxon clean-up crews set up camp wherever they could. They rushed to establish facilities in shops that catered to tourists, a drug store, a museum, a library, a school, and a small post office. The only place large enough for the Exxon Command Center was the second floor of a building called Valdez Chiropractic Center and Teddy Bear Day Care. Public Affairs was set up on the second floor over a Department Store; *Exxon Valdez* employees used offices at the building of the National Bank of Alaska so technicians handling radios could keep in touch with people in cleanup areas. The boat harbor previously used for the fishing industry was used to bring in supplies.

People outside of the oil industry were also hired for cleanup. Workers lived in homes opened to them by locals, in portable home-camps set up by Exxon, in hotels, and on hotel ships docked in the port (referred to as "flotels"). One fast-food company, Burger King, opened in a portable building. Working and living conditions were reported to have bordered on primitive—like camping in the wilderness. As the months passed and summer came, the number of sunlight hours in Alaska increased to 22 hours each day, decreasing the number of hours workers were comfortably able to sleep. Exxon Valdez cleanup crews often had shifts of 12-18 hours per day, 7 days a week, sometimes for 30-day stretches.

The sea tossed the oil so far onto the land that trees along the shoreline were coated 6-8 feet high with oil. Work on the front line was hazardous, as oil-covered rocks were slippery. Safety became simply about watching one's step. Media outlets displayed disturbing images of dead whales and otters floating in the oil-soaked ocean and blackened birds gasping for breath on the shore. Wildlife rescue centers were busy trying to keep oil-soaked shore birds and sea otters alive. Supplies and equipment had to be flown, trucked or barged in. Some areas were barely accessible. Local Eskimos were seen making futile attempts at cleaning the oil off the shoreline with rags.

Ironically, Jack was in the Exxon Valdez clean-up zone on the day that marked the 10th anniversary of his own boat mishap, the sinking of the *Ramona R.* and his own experience as a boat captain. That was a life-altering experience for Jack, but as reports came in that the captain of the *Exxon Valdez* was accused of not being in control of the ship when it ran aground and Exxon was blamed for not having a better plan in place for an accident of this type, Jack was thankful his loss affected only himself and a slight inconvenience to the coast guard and the town of Ft. Bragg. The *Exxon Valdez* spill was destructive to the entire community, wildlife, the environment, businesses, captain and crew. While the clean-up was underway, people protested and boycotted Exxon stations. The Exxon Corporation was also under scrutiny because for many years they had assured the public that drilling for oil in Prudhoe Bay would not damage the environment. They were also accused of downplaying the negative aspects of the clean-up as well.

In the end, one million barrels of oil were removed from the Exxon Valdez, and the ship was refloated. By September, the shoreline was somewhat cleaner, and the wildlife appeared to be in recovery mode. The *Exxon Valdez* oil spill was considered the largest, most destructive oil spill in U.S. history, and world-wide media coverage was extensive. The spill changed the way many people, including Jack, thought about the safety of the oil pipeline.

Little Jackie Smith Became...

CHAPTER NINE
Well-traveled

While living and working at the clean-up zone of the Exxon Valdez, Jack applied for a job as a CAG, the acronym for a Cleared American Guard — not to be confused with the CAG, the U.S. Army's Combat Applications Group, also known as Delta Force; Jack was a healthy and motivated fifty-year-old man, but he wasn't quite that ambitious. Rather, the Cleared American Guard was a position title for security personnel assigned to construction sites at U.S. embassies around the world. Jack liked the idea of spending time in other countries with exposure to people with cultures different than his own, and the job would allow Jack to continue to earn decent wages at the type of work he enjoyed.

In February 1990, six months after Jack left his job in Alaska, he passed through a top security clearance background investigation and was offered a job offer as a CAG — and he accepted. So, just a few months later, in the summer of 1990, Jack stored his photos from Prudhoe Bay, Alaska, and a VHS tape from the cleanup of the Exxon Valdez spill into his Samsonite, secured it in his storage unit in Oroville, and traveled to Washington D.C. for Cleared American Guard training. A short time later, he was sent on his first assignment — Belgrade, Yugoslavia, where he worked alongside U.S. Marines in protecting a construction site within the U.S. Embassy.

In Jack's first letter to Alan and Vickie, he described how his employer-provided living and working accommodations were simple and very comfortable—just the way he liked it. He wrote about the embassy:

> Only part of it is being renovated so it's still fully staffed including the marine detachment. It's a large multi-story complex and we have our own recreation center, bar, dining facilities, and commissary. Many personnel from other embassies come here to eat, drink, and socialize because theirs have little or none.

Jack wrote about how he enjoyed walking to and from his apartment and the U.S. Embassy, mostly so he could pass through the city and people watch. He wrote:

> I enjoy getting out and about on foot as there's a lot to see. We all live 4-6 miles from the embassy in apartments. I share one with another guard and a company's vehicle transports us back and forth. On nice days, I like to walk in just to watch the hustle and bustle.

Jack commented on the city of Belgrade having a population of 1.6 million—a lot more people than he was typically comfortable with, but he also knew his job there was temporary, so he decided to enjoy it for the time. The man who preferred the small-town feel wrote, "It's a nice place to visit, but that's it."

One of the reasons Jack wanted to work overseas was for the cultural experience, and he wrote home to tell about one of his discoveries, saying of the Serbians, "…they're a very curious lot."

Jack told the story of how, on several occasions, he had been window shopping alone, and within a couple of minutes of stopping to look at merchandise in a window, he was surrounded, and even pushed aside, by people wanting to get a look at whatever Jack found so interesting. At first, Jack got somewhat annoyed at their rudeness, but then he found it amusing. Jack also told the story of standing in a spot looking at his watch while at the flea market, and how 4-5 curious people surrounded him and helped him look at his watch – one person even asked him how much he wanted for it. Jack wrote, "Now, I don't mean to demean or belittle these good folks. I guess everywhere people have certain quirks, and this just happens to be theirs."

Two months later, Jack was excited to tell his children that he had been invited to the local Marine Corps Ball. His children were surprised that he seemed excited to go, since their dad was rarely one to attend functions that required him to dress in formal attire, because when not in work uniform, Jack preferred to wear a white t-shirt underneath a short-sleeved, plaid shirt, all of which were tucked into casual pants secured with a belt – he was rarely seen without also wearing simple socks and a comfortable pair of shoes. But Jack was thrilled at having been invited to such a historical event in U.S. military history, and he didn't think twice about going.

*The Marine Security Guard Detachment
Belgrade, Yugoslavia
requests the pleasure of your company
at the 215th Marine Corps Birthday Ball
to be held at the
Crystal Ballroom, Hyatt Regency Hotel
on 10 November, 1990 at 18,00 hours*

*5 Milentija Popovica   Attire: Civilian-Formal
New Belgrade   Military Dress 'A'*

1990 Marine Corps Birthday Ball invitation

So, on the evening of November 10, 1990, Jack dressed in his Sunday best and went to the Hyatt Regency Hotel in Belgrade to attend the 215th Marine Corps Birthday Ball.

While Jack was settling into his new job and getting accustomed to his environment in Belgrade, he wrote to his children about the government in Yugoslavia and how the people were dealing with intense political issues, including suspicion of voter fraud and accusations that Serbian-controlled media had been intentionally reporting false information. People opposed to communism began planning demonstrations. Jack wrote:

Seems they were not allowed access to the government-controlled media to state their platform or rebuke allegations, plus the various forms of threats and intimidations they and their supporters were subjected to, a demonstration was planned to air these and other complaints. The Serbian Government warned that force would be used if they did. The answer, in effect, was "hide and watch."

A few months later, on Saturday, March 9, 1991, word spread that personnel at the U.S. Embassy should avoid downtown Belgrade during specific periods of time because of planned political demonstrations. The flier given to Jack contained the following typewritten message:

ALL PEOPLE WHO WANT PEACE IN OUR COUNTRY AND IN WHOLE WORLD, WHO ARE AGAINST WAR AND BLOODSHED, ARE INVITED TO COME TO AN ANTI-WAR NON-PARTY GATHERING NEAR THE DELIJSKA FOUNTAIN IN KNEZ MIHAJLOVA STREET, ON SATURDAY, JULY 6 AT 17:00.

LET THE MESSAGE FROM ALL OF US BE: GIVE A CHANCE TO PEACE!

YOUTH OF BELGRADE

Jack's supervisor handwrote a note below the typed mes-

ALL PEOPLE WHO WANT PEACE IN OUR COUNTRY AND IN WHOLE WORLD,
WHO ARE AGAINST WAR AND BLOODSHED, ARE INVITED TO COME TO AN
ANTI-WAR, NON-PARTY GATHERING NEAR THE DELIJSKA FOUNTAIN IN
KNEZ MIHAJLOVA STREET, ON SATURDAY, JULY 6 AT 17:00.

LET THE MESSAGE FROM ALL OF US BE:
                    GIVE A CHANCE TO PEACE!

                              YOUTH OF BELGRADE

Youth of Belgrade flier

sage: There will be a demonstration on Knez Mihajlova Street on Saturday July 6 at 5PM. Please avoid downtown Belgrade from 3PM until Sunday morning."

By 2:45 P.M. on Sunday, there was no word of anyone protesting, and the thrill-seeker in Jack was getting anxious to see what was, or was not, going on, so he headed into downtown

Belgrade for what he called a "look-see." On foot, Jack made his way from the embassy, located only eight blocks from the center of town. About four blocks in, he noticed the tempo of the pedestrian traffic starting to pick up. One block closer, he could hear sounds of periodic roars. Jack said in a whisper, "Hot damn, the party's on!"

After winding through a few more side streets and alleys, Jack rounded a corner and came upon thousands of people, so he looked around for an escape route in case of need for a quick retreat. Jack found an observation spot on the outer fringe of the mass of people, and later wrote home that he "...just took in the whole spectacle of a real, live demonstration against communist suppression."

Minutes later, Jack heard sounds of muffled pops, and the down-wind position was suddenly covered with tear gas fumes. Jack's eyes were watery, and his throat and nose were burning as he and others near him quickly cleared the area. Once Jack was safely away from the main crowd, he went in search of the troopers. Jack took a few side streets in semi-circle fashion and he happened upon part of a backup unit dressed in full vests, helmets, gas masks, shields and clubs. There were also about two dozen riot police standing around two water cannon tankers.

A short time later, Jack saw a group of protestors handing out free Marlboro cigarettes. That was Jack's brand, so he excitedly, but politely, made his way into the crowd in hopes of getting some free smokes. Unfortunately, by the time he made it to the front of the group, they had run out of cigarettes. Jack thought, "Oh well. It was a great idea if nothing else." He watched the demonstrations for a while longer, and without further incident, went home for the night.

The following day, about 500 demonstrators gathered but were then dispersed. That night, college students came out to support the opposition party against the Serbian government and Federal government's actions. The protestors organized in two locations, and within hours there were 7000 people near the main part of the city and another 3000 to 5000 across the Sava River—locations of student dorms. The police blocked the bridge crossing the Sava River so the students couldn't cross over and join with the city group. Jack seemed excited for the students when he wrote in a letter to a friend:

> Well lo and behold if a few hundred of the city's 3000 cab drivers didn't cross over another bridge, load up all the students they could, then returning 3 abreast right through town, horns blaring, kids chanting and hanging out and hanging on. Got most of them joined up and free of charge to boot. Monday the student protests got into full swing—this time no interference from the authorities.

Later, the university students were joined by high school students and the original groups of demonstrators. The protest lasted around the clock until Wednesday when Slobodan Milosevic, the Serbian president, met most of their demands and things calmed—at least temporarily. During the five-day melee, however, two people died and many more were injured. Less than two weeks later, Jack bought a *Newsweek* magazine, which reported on the events he witnessed in Belgrade, the history of the political strife, and predictions of where it would lead. The *Newsweek* story was titled, "This Is Just the Beginning."

Three months later, smaller, periodic incidents of unrest continued to the point that a foreign diplomat requested the help of CAG personnel to conduct surveillance around his home overnight. Embassy security supervisors recommended Jack, so in June 1991, he reported for duty at the diplomatic housing community in Belgrade. The diplomat he was assisting discussed recent burglaries and thefts in the area, and at 9:45 P.M., he and Jack walked around his residence and a wooded area nearby. At 10 P.M., armed with a flashlight, binoculars, and a radio, Jack took up a post and began surveillance. At 2 A.M., with no unusual traffic or activities in the area, Jack's surveillance ended for the night, and a patrol vehicle retuned him to his own residence.

Jack returned to the diplomatic housing community over the next five nights where he notified local vehicle patrol of any cars entering the area where he approached and shined his flashlight in windows of those that parked nearby, particularly in unlit areas. He watched as pedestrians entered and exited the areas, and along with officers from the local vehicle patrol units, he confronted and helped identify trespassers. On night six, Jack was nearing the end of his shift when he noticed a male and a female riding a red scooter toward him. When they noticed Jack standing near the street, they turned around and sped off. Jack radioed the nearby vehicle patrol who then followed the scooter until it departed the area. The remainder of Jack's shift was uneventful.

Though technology had advanced since Jack worked as a deputy in the 1960s and 1970s, and Jack was fully trained in all technological requirements needed to do his job, in the early nineties, there was still an obvious need for good, old-fashioned human surveillance combined with the simple physical presence of a security officer as a crime deterrent. In less than one week of nightly foot patrol duties, the diplomat no longer feared being burglarized, so Jack returned to the U.S. Embassy for his usual work shifts.

As Jack's first year of employment as a Cleared American Guard was nearing an end in Belgrade, he was evaluated. Jack's supervisor wrote:

> Mr. Smith has always maintained a professional attitude and could always be relied upon. He participated actively within the Embassy com-munity and has been an asset to the Embassy, as well as the Construction Security Program. Smith has a positive attitude toward mission accomplishment and is quick to make suggest-ions that are helpful. Smith is active in the em-bassy community as a member of the Commissary Board, the American Club Financial Board, and is active in the CLO. I would recommend Mr. Smith for increased responsibility and look forward to working with him in the future.

In July 1991, with high recommendations from his superiors, Jack prepared to return to Oroville until he received his next work assignment. Before he left Belgrade, however, a note on a half-sheet of paper was left for him. It read, "Please give it to Mr. Jack Smith." The note was signed by Satoshi, a man Jack had befriended while in Belgrade. Under an arrow pointing from Satoshi's name was an image, hand-drawn in thin, blue ink, depicting a man wearing glasses and a striped suit; he was smiling and holding a briefcase. The word "Japanese" was written beside the image. In addition to the note was a yellow Post-it with an image, hand-drawn in thick, blue ink, depicting a face with thick hair, dark facial features, and a square jawline. The words "Jack Smith from U.S.A." was written next to the image.

One month later, after spending time with family and friends in Oroville and Sacramento, Jack reported for his next U.S. Embassy assignment—Moscow. He arrived to find a political climate as unstable as the one he witnessed in Belgrade; the difference, however, was that in Belgrade it was those who opposed communism who were making their voices heard, but in Moscow, it was the hardline members of the Communist Party, the most supportive of communism, who were challenging the government and creating an uproar. These staunch communists were upset with Soviet President Mikhail Gorbachev because they believed his policies were putting communist ideals at risk and causing the economy to crumble.

On August 19, 1991, shortly after Jack arrived in Moscow, matters worsened. A few high-ranking Communist Party government officials attempted to carry out a coup d'état; they held Soviet president Mikhail Gorbachev on house arrest and planned to arrest and imprison the newly elected Russian president, Boris Yeltsin. The coup plotters made a radio announcement that an Emergency Committee was going to govern the Soviet Union; however, there was no follow up to their announcement—while people waited to hear updates, the radio simply played hours of music from the Swan Lake ballet.

In the meantime, civilians crowded around Russia's parliament building where, by August 21, fights broke out, and the military and police were called in to maintain order. Soldiers and tanks filled the streets, shots were fired, and at least three people were killed in the chaos. Jack and other personnel at the U.S. Embassy were asked to avoid the area and as a measure of security, a small side-street leading from the parliament building to the U.S. Embassy was lined with diplomats' cars to form a barricade.

On August 22, the coup attempt failed. Mikhail Gorbachev was released from house arrest, and Boris Yeltsin remained free. The U.S. Embassy was within walking distance from the action, so once the dust cleared, Jack made his way to the parliament building. There, he took pictures of Soviet tanks, soldiers, crowds still forming, and dozens of flowers that lay in memory of those who lost their lives.

A week after the failed coup d'état, communist supporters' last desperate attempt at saving the Union of Soviet Socialist Republics, the first of many republics declared independence. Days later, more Soviet-controlled republics gained independence, and declarations of independence continued over the next few months. Then, on Christmas Day 1991, Mikhail Gorbachev appeared on satellite television and resigned as Soviet president. Airing live on ITN television, a news anchor's opening statement reported the end of seven decades of communist rule in the Soviet Union, and the news host announced, "Gorbachev, the last president of the Soviet Union, resigns." In his televised statement, Mikhail Gorbachev said, in part, "Compatriots, due to the situation which has evolved as a result of the formation of the commonwealth of independent states, I hereby discontinue my activities at the post of president of the USSR...this society has acquired freedom. It has been freed politically and spiritually, and this is the most important achievement that we have yet to fully come to grips with, and we haven't because we haven't learned to use freedom yet."

The Soviet Union was no more—in large part due to the work done during the presidency of Jack's old acquaintance, Ronald Reagan. Boris Yeltsin remained president of the newly established independent Russian state, and that evening at the Kremlin, less than two miles from where Jack was working at the U.S. Embassy, Yeltsin ordered the Soviet hammer and sickle flag be lowered for a final time, and the Russian flag was raised. There were only a few people in the square to witness the event. It was reported that the crowd was small and unexpectedly quiet; no one appeared happy, yet no one appeared sad either.

Coincidentally, on the same day in the United States, Jack's grandchildren opened gifts mailed to them from Moscow by their Grandpa Jack. In large and small packages, they pulled out jewelry, clothing, toys, and stuffed animals, all made in Russia. Those aware of the major developments having occurred in Moscow on the same day wondered if the items were intended to be gifts or souvenirs. Knowing Jack, it was likely both.

On Christmas night, U.S. President George H.W. Bush, announced on television in that the Soviet Union had officially collapsed. The next morning, *The New York Times* described the historic day in an article titled, "Gorbachev, Last Soviet Leader, Resigns; U.S. Recognizes Republics' Independence."

While the Soviet Bloc was dismantling, Jack and his colleagues knew they had to continue their work as usual. Prior to Jack's arrival in Moscow, he had been informed that the Russian government had been caught, on numerous occasions, bugging buildings inside the U.S. Embassy — even as recently as three years earlier. Some of the bugging incidents occurred in buildings under construction, and three months after Jack's assignment began, his keen observation skills may have helped to deter a crime in progress on the grounds of the U.S. Embassy. While on his shift, Jack reported unusual activity near a warehouse where materials from Helsinki were being unloaded and stored. He spotted three individuals inside a building under construction; the building was usually empty inside, so Jack notified his supervisor of what he observed. When Jack's shift ended 30 minutes later, he informed his replacement who later informed Jack that the individuals must have left the building because no further activity was observed.

Two months later, in January 1992, even though the Cold War was said to be over, Jack and his colleagues knew the untrustworthy tactics by the Russian government were not going to end immediately. In fact, on at least one occasion, while working at the U.S. Embassy, Jack's body began to feel hot. He suspected he was being exposed to radiation or something of that sort. So, Jack remained vigilant. One night, he reported for a his shift beginning at 7 P.M. Jack and a coworker were informed by the staff they were relieving that a gate needed to be opened earlier in the day for snow removal, but the key bent and was stuck inside the security padlock. The officers on duty decided to cut the lock off and replace it with a smaller, temporary lock from the security office until a stronger, more efficient security padlock could be obtained.

Jack didn't find the broken lock unusual, particularly because it was likely the result of frigid weather conditions, but he was concerned when he saw a bent key, still on the key ring, and the broken lock sitting in a trash can. Jack looked for log entries regarding the discarded lock but found nothing. He checked to see if a report had been written about the change of locks, but there was none. Jack later wrote that he was, "...concerned over the fact that the incident had not been handled in the best interest of security procedures."

When Jack reported the incident to his supervisor, his concerns were dismissed; Jack was treated as though he was overreacting, but he stood his ground. Jack was not a man who took shortcuts. He understood that the discarded lock may have appeared to be minor incident, but proper protocol needed to be followed regardless so that minor issues didn't allow for or contribute to a major problem—especially considering the tense and unstable environment he and his coworkers were surrounded by in Moscow.

Not everyone, however, believed the discarded lock and key was as important as Jack did. In fact, in less-than-kind words, Jack was told that if he was so concerned about the discarded padlock incident, he should just write the report himself. So, being a man who was known for his attention to detail, Jack did write and submit the incident report. Jack also wrote a documented account of the encounter with his supervisor as well, and he saved it just in case it was needed for future reference.

Jack enjoyed roaming about the city of Moscow. He was impressed with the metro system—particularly how modern and efficient it was in accommodating the city's population of 10 million people. Jack also enjoyed the people of Moscow, and as he made his way around the city, on foot, he got a good laugh out of watching some of the older Russian women walk along the streets and, when needed, simply shove people aside to get to their destination. On several occasions, he also passed by street vendor sketch-artists whose artwork reminded Jack of the landscapes his mom drew with charcoal when he was a child. Though Jack didn't typically go out of his way to have his image drawn (or even his photo taken, for that matter), in honor of his mother's memory, he decided to become a subject for the artist. Jack also gave the street vendor a picture of Vickie, and a sketch was drawn of her as well.

A year earlier, Jack had purchased a video camera, so be-

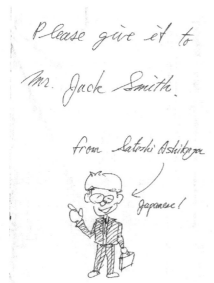

Drawings by Jack's friend, Satoshi, Belgrade, Yugoslavia, 1991

Christmas photo of Jack, Vickie, and Courtney displaying Russian street vendor drawing of Vickie over fireplace mantle, mid-1990s

fore his Moscow assignment ended in the summer of 1992, he decided to capture footage of various locations within the city. One thing Jack made sure to get on video was the memorial established in honor of those who were killed near the parliament building during the days-long coup attempt that occurred when he first arrived in Moscow.

When Jack returned to Oroville, he had a collection of foreign and domestic mementoes. He also had video recordings and photos of some of the cities he worked in and the European cities he visited, but he didn't have pictures of himself in any of those places. Outside of the photo on each of his name badges, the only images of Jack had of himself from his overseas work were drawn, first in Belgrade by his Japanese friend, Satoshi, and then in Moscow by the street vendor sketch artist. Each was given a home inside Jack's Samsonite.

Little Jackie Smith Became…

CHAPTER TEN
A Friend

In the mid-1990s, Jack resigned from his position as a Clear-ed American Guard. Having been away from his family and friends for the better part of 11 years, Jack experienced all of Alan's and Vickie's high school years through letters, cards, short visits, and brief phone calls. For the most part, that was also Jack's experience in his children's lives through the four years Alan spent in the Army prior to becoming a computer programmer, and during Vickie's involvement in the music business before she enrolled in college. Jack wanted to be closer so he could share in more of the lives Alan and Vickie were building in Sacramento, and at times, he worried about them. For years, Jack had given his children financial and moral support, but as adults, they no longer needed his financial assistance, so instead, he wanted to be physically present for them.

Jack was also ready to settle back into a simple life again. He believed he got his fill of excitement large cities in foreign countries with political turmoil could offer — particularly after the night he was walking along a busy street in Rome, just about midnight, when Jack saw a bright flash of light a few yards away. The light was immediately followed by a loud sound and the pressure of an explosion. Glass and other debris began to shower upon Jack, so, with his ears ringing, he threw his tote bag over his head and dashed around the corner of the building.

Jack wrote to Alan and Vickie. He described the moment the explosion occurred. Jack wrote, "Being right about 54 years old, I had no difficulty performing a crouched, long-stride dash. I attribute this to; (1) fear is the actuator of agility and speed; (2) I was entering the phenomenon of flight or fright; or (3) I found out just how fast scared is. My choice: all of the above."

A minute or so later, Jack peeked around the building. He saw a nearby car and a building on fire, electrical wires were strewn about and made popping sounds, and other buildings and some historical structures were crumbling. Glass and other debris covered the ground and any vehicles parked in the area. It didn't take long to realize someone had set off a car bomb, something Jack described as, "...a dramatic, intriguing, Holy Sh—episode." Jack ended the letter to his children by stating, "Ol' dad's on another adventure."

Jack decided to settle down back in Oroville again—quickly realizing it wasn't the exact same town he moved out of in 1982. One difference was the population growth, but, unfortunately, not due to an increase in job opportunities—in some ways Oroville was still in a recovery mode from the recession of the seventies. There had been some commercial growth from the seventies through the nineties; a few building renovations in town, the establishment of a casino on local Native American land, and upgrades in road conditions and the occasional road expansion to accommodate the increasing population. Sadly, without enough jobs to sustain the increase in population, poverty was more apparent, and so too were signs of the destructive increase in methamphetamine abuse.

There were, however, some positive aspects about Oroville that remained, like the simple, laid-back atmosphere, the sense of community, and the overwhelming number of genuinely good-hearted people. Evidence of this occurred in 1982 when white supremacist activity at Oroville High School resulted in the murder of a young man. People of the town responded by marching through the streets, in the thousands, to oppose racism, the Ku Klux Klan, and Neo-Nazism in Oroville. They were not going to allow hatred, bigotry, and violence to dominate their town.

Jack's friendships also remained strong while he was working in Alaska and overseas. Jack grew up with very few blood-family members in his life, so developing relationships with people who were not blood-relatives became an important part of his life. When he returned to live in Oroville again, those friendships picked up as though he had never left.

One of those friends was Tony DeAngelo, who, in the 1970s, was a bartender at Prospector's Village. Located on Oro Dam Boulevard – the main strip in Oroville – Prospector's Village was an upscale motel equipped with the largest bar in town, a restaurant, a dance floor, banquet halls, and live music. On Jack's days off from work as a deputy, he would often sit at the bar to keep his friend company during the slow times, usually during daytime hours. Jack drank coffee, and would stick around until the evening crowd arrived and would be long gone before people at the bar got wild or started jumping from the roof of Prospector's Village into the pool, just outside the bar.

After Jack's retirement from the Sheriff's Department, he started working at Prospector's Village, alongside his friend, Tony. Later, the two men considered investing in business together, first in Panama and then in Missouri, but neither venture worked out. When Jack returned to Oroville from working overseas at U.S. embassies, Tony was the manager of a housing community near the Feather River. Jack and Tony, both single men at the time, shared a home on the property. Though Jack earned an income as a courier and delivery driver, he helped cover his portion of the rent with landscaping duties each week. Jack enjoyed riding the mower on the large grassy area around the housing community.

When Jack wasn't at his home (and calling Alan and Vickie to brag about the hours-long smell of Tony's home-made spaghetti sauce cooking on the stovetop and antici-pating the addition of Tony's homemade meatballs), his spare time was often spent having coffee with a group of other friends at Jack's favorite diner. Jack and his friends met at noon and 5 P.M. each day, sometimes just to have coffee, sometimes for coffee and a snack, and sometimes coffee and a meal — but always coffee and always to shoot the breeze. Jack also enjoyed spending time scrolling through books of interest at the local library. It wasn't long after returning to Oroville from his time away in Alaska and working overseas before Jack fell back into a comfortable routine.

Living in Oroville again, Jack was easily able to drive to Sacramento to spend time with his growing family, mostly on holidays and birthdays, and his children and grandchildren traveled to Oroville to see him as well. Alan was married and worked for a magazine publishing company. Vickie was married with three daughters, taught childbirth classes several evenings each week at local hospitals, and she attended college classes during the day. Jack was thrilled to see his children excelling in their lives, and because he always impressed upon his children the importance of higher education, he enjoyed listening to Vickie describe her experience in college. Jack excitedly watched Vickie's progress in college, as she inched her way closer to a bachelor's degree, and though no one knew it at the time, Jack would actually become part of Vickie's college experience.

In June 1996, Vickie's school assignment prompted her to share her family history. She was close to her mom's family, so that information was relatively easy to find. She knew, from her childhood, a few of her dad's paternal relatives: her Grandpa Smitty, his sister, Gracie, and their brother, George—relatives from Jack's Missouri-based family. Getting information about Jack's mother, Victoria, and her family, however, was much more difficult. When Vickie was young, Jack told her his mother was of French and Italian ancestry and that her French immigrant father was highly educated and could speak several languages. Jack also told Vickie his mother committed suicide by jumping off a building top when he was a young boy; he missed her so much that when Vickie was born, he named her in honor of his mother. Jack had shown Vickie and Alan pictures of his mother when they were in their early teens, and a few years later, Jack gave

Vickie the signet ring with his initials engraved on it that his mother had given to him before she died. Every day after that, Vickie wore the ring on her right ring finger, but Victoria was rarely discussed.

As a college student, Vickie wanted to know more about her grandmother, Victoria, and the family history class assignment seemed like, to her, the perfect opportunity to ask some questions. As far as Vickie was concerned, she could only go to one person to get more information about Victoria—and that person was her dad. At first, Vickie wondered if Jack spoke so little of his mother over the years because doing so was too painful for him, and she feared raising the topic might cause her dad to relive difficult childhood memories. Vickie knew, however, that Jack was excited about her pursuit of higher education because in the seventies, he, too, worked toward a college degree—maybe her dad would understand what led her to ask.

Vickie never knew her dad to hide in fear from anything, but she also didn't know how deep the wounds from his childhood may be—and she certainly did not want to be the one to open those wounds—so Vickie decided she would approach the topic lightly to see what Jack's initial reaction was, and then she would have a feel for whether it was a good idea to continue or not. One day Jack received a call from Vickie. The conversation started out the same as the weekly conversation they usually had, and when Vickie felt it was safe, she talked to Jack about her family history class assignment. Vickie told her dad that she hoped he would give her some information about his mother. To Vickie's relief,

Jack replied, "Yeah, that sounds good."

Jack told Vickie as much as he could remember about his childhood. Smitty left Oatman, Arizona, shortly after Jack was born, so Jack and his mom moved to Fresno, California, to be near her family. Jack's mom was unable to financially care for him on her own, so Jack told Vickie about living in the foster homes during the week and seeing his mom on weekends. Jack spoke of fun at the foster homes and times when he visited his mom's family and got to play with his cousins. Jack told Vickie that, at the time, he was called Jackie, and sometimes Little Jackie.

As Jack told Vickie stories about his mom and the times they spent together, Vickie noticed his voiced softened, and he was nothing but complimentary about his mother. At times, he repeated the word "Mom" so many times, Vickie imagined him as a little boy telling stories about a mother he adored. Vickie also realized that her dad's thrill-seeking side started when he was a child; Jack talked of going to the community pool with his mom and how he would jump into the deep end, then wait at the bottom of the pool until someone jumped into rescue him while his mom screamed in panic.

Jack described his mom as liking the outdoors, and that she was a good freehand artist who liked to draw landscapes in charcoal. Jack also told Vickie about the times he spent with his mother at the theatre, and when the orchestra played during intermission his mom always requested the orchestra to play "Blue Moon." Jack said, "It was her favorite song." Vickie was familiar with the song, "Blue Moon," mostly be-

Jack as an infant with his mother

Jack as a toddler

Jack, preschool age, in the front yard of his first foster home.

Jack, preschool age, on his mom's lap in the front yard of his first foster home

cause it was in her favorite childhood movie, *Grease* — she saw the movie ten times during the summer it was released, and as an eleven-year old, she played the soundtrack album on a record player at home for hours at a time while attempting to reenact some of the dance scenes. In the early eighties, *Blue Moon* was included on the soundtrack of the movie *An American Werewolf in London*, and in the mid-1990s, the movie *Apollo 13*, but nothing reminded Vickie of the song quite like the movie, *Grease*.

Vickie thought *Blue Moon* originated in the 1950s, but learning that it had already been released and popular by the time her dad was a child in the forties, that it was Victoria's favorite song, and that Victoria requested the song be played when she was hanging out with her son, Vickie believed the song must have represented Victoria's love for Jackie. That's when Vickie, who shared a name with Victoria, realized she had something else in common with her grandmother: Vickie also had a favorite song which represented her love for Jack.

When Vickie and Alan were young, they believed everyone in town knew their dad. Jack would take his children to his favorite diner, and upon entering, Jack would be greeted by the wait-staff (like Norm on *Cheers*, but not in unison — and long before *Cheers* was created.) After sitting in a booth at the diner, people passing their table would often stop and want to talk to Jack. A visitor would claim to only be stopping for a minute, but while Alan and Vickie waited under a veil of cigarette smoke, the conversation would often last much longer than expected. Jack was never one who talked much, he mostly listened and offered agreement, compliment, consolation, or confirmation — and always with a smile.

When one person walked away, another would approach and talk to Jack — individuals and couples alike. They were all friendly, and Jack would always stand to greet them and shake their hands. Before departing, the visitors would remind Alan and Vickie of what a good man Jack was, and how lucky they were to have him as their father. With a mouthful of pancakes and hashed browns, and while sipping chocolate milk from a straw, Alan and Vickie were bashful, but each looked at their dad and proudly displayed a goofy, closed-mouth smile. The constant barrage of visitors didn't bother Alan and Vickie because when they were alone, Jack made sure to give them his undivided attention. Plus, they were proud to be with someone like their dad, the kindest man they knew, and apparently, to them, the most popular guy in town.

Because of the amount of public attention Jack received, when Vickie was seven-years old, she associated lyrics from the song *(They Long to be) Close to You* with her dad. In addition to believing the angels really did get together to create a dream come true the day her dad was born, Vickie also felt as if birds and stars appeared when he was near, and as far as she could tell, all the girls (and guys) in town — maybe not all, but certainly a lot — followed her dad around because, like Vickie, and Alan too, they wanted to be close to Jack.

Vickie was fine with knowing that some of the lyrics of the song did not apply to her dad; he didn't have gold hair or blue eyes, he had dark features, but in Vickie's eyes, the lyrics that *did* apply to him fit perfectly. Vickie would sing along to the

Carpenter's best-of album titled *Singles* on a record player at home and whenever *(They Long to be) Close to You* played, she would sing along as though she was singing about her dad. Then, during the horn solo, she imagined dancing with her dad in a ballroom-style, father-daughter dance, spotlighted in a room full of people—maybe as a way of reminding herself that even though others might take her dad's attention for a short time, when it came to his children, the focus of Jack's love was unquestionable.

When Vickie was older, she realized the song *(They Long to be) Close to You* was probably written with romantic intent, but that didn't change things. In Vickie's mind, the lyrics applied to love between a parent and a child, the same as Victoria had likely done with the meaning of the lyrics to the song *Blue Moon*, and as an adult, whenever Vickie heard *(They Long to be) Close to You*, it brought back memories and the love she had for her dad as a child. It made Vickie smile because even as an adult, she continued to adore him the same.

Vickie never told anyone about the image she created to *(They Long to be) Close to You*, and how she thought it represented her dad. She didn't even tell Jack the day he talked about his mom and her favorite song, *Blue Moon*. Vickie didn't say a word to her dad about it, she just smiled at knowing how she and her grandmother had found a similar way of associating their feelings for the same person, and Vickie let her dad continue telling stories from his childhood.

According to Jack, everything changed when he was eight years old and his dad appeared in Fresno. Jack's parents reunited, he was taken out of foster care, and they lived as a family. At first, everything seemed to be going well, until, that is, Smitty started disappearing again—sometimes in short spurts but other times for days on end. As a result, Jack said his mom became sad and sometimes anxious, and each time Smitty disappeared, Victoria's emotional state worsened. She became violent toward Smitty when he returned, and occasionally, she turned her aggression toward Jackie. Victoria's behavior was unpredictable—one minute she seemed as calm as she normally was, the next minute she seemed crazy, and then she would snap back into normal behavior without memory of having hit Smitty or Jackie.

Jack explained that it was Victoria's erratic and violent behavior that led to her arrest and placement in a mental hospital when he was ten years old. At the time, they were living in Sacramento, and after Victoria was taken by police, Smitty took Jackie to visit his mom twice in the mental facility. Jack didn't remember where it was, he only remembered it being a hospital at the top of a hill. Before Victoria was released from the hospital, Smitty moved Jackie to Southern California, and a few months later, in the driveway of the home in which they were living, Jackie was sitting in a car with Smitty, and that's when Jackie was told his mother was dead.

Days later, Smitty took Jackie back to Fresno for Victoria's funeral. Because Victoria's sisters had blamed Smitty for the suicide, when they saw him, they tried to attack him. Victoria's brother took Jackie outside so he wouldn't witness the chaos. A few minutes later, Smitty came out of the funeral home, took his son's hand, and the two of them left. Sadly,

Jackie didn't get to attend his mother's funeral. A couple of days later, Smitty took Jackie to meet with Victoria's dad on a street corner where Smitty was offered money to leave Jackie with relatives in Fresno, and for Smitty to disappear. Smitty refused, walked away with his son, and they left Fresno.

Vickie obtained enough information from her dad that day to complete her class assignment, but not enough to satisfy her personal quest. Some of Vickie's initial questions were answered, but in the process of obtaining those answers, even more questions were raised. For example, Vickie told her dad she was happy to know the foster families treated him well, but she was very curious about why Victoria lived in the same city as her parents and her adult siblings, most of whom had families of their own, but Little Jackie still had to live in a foster home. Jack told Vickie that he always wondered that too.

Jack also wondered about something his mother once pointed out to him. When Jack was young, his mom took him to the front of an office building and told him that if anything were to happen to her, "Remember this man's name and this place." As an adult, Jack could not remember the man's name or the place. He told Vickie he thought the man may have been an attorney or that his mother may have taken out an insurance policy or something to that effect—but he couldn't recall. Vickie wondered if that was a reason her dad kept so many memorabilia in his adult life—maybe as reminders, so he was less likely to forget important details of his past.

Throughout Vickie's life, when she was seeking answers and sought advice from her dad, he taught her to pay attention to detail, and to follow her gut. Vickie applied that advice when researching her dad's childhood, and her gut was telling her there were details missing and she needed to find them. Vickie asked if her dad was okay with her searching for historical documents. Jack gave his blessing and said he would help in anyway he could. Vickie also suggested trying to locate members of Victoria's family for more information. Jack told her about his attempt to do the same when Alan was an infant (before Vickie's birth) and their family stopped in Fresno on their way to Tijuana, Mexico, how they visited the home of his mother's sister, Grace, and her young-adult daughter, Linda, and that Grace gave Jack pictures of him from his childhood, many with his mother, but answered very few questions. Jack told Vickie that, after Vickie's birth, he sent Grace pictures of his newborn daughter, but they lost contact shortly after that.

Vickie said she would give it shot, too, so Jack gave her his mother's maiden name, Lazar, and any of the other relatives' first names that he could remember. Using the Fresno City Directory, Vickie started out by making phone calls to those listed under the Lazar name. The first person she reached, a young man, didn't know of a family member named Victoria, so he suggested Vickie call his dad. The young man's dad said he had an aunt, Victoria, and she died when he was young, but she didn't have any children. Vickie was quick to correct him that Victoria did indeed have a son, she said, "His name is Jack; they called him Jackie." The man suggested Vickie call his aunt Grace, Victoria's oldest sister — the same person Jack visited in Fresno the year before Vickie's birth and who Jack stayed in contact with until shortly after Vickie was born. Vickie called Grace, and when she realized who Vickie was, Grace said, "I can probably tell you when your birthday is. I still write your birthday on my calendar."

Grace spoke of how deeply Victoria loved Jackie, and according to Grace, Victoria treated Jackie like a king. When Smitty abandoned them (he allegedly ran off with another woman) in Oatman, Arizona, Victoria carried Jackie in her arms and hitchhiked through the Mojave Desert — all the way to her parent's home in Fresno, California. While hitchhiking, Victoria shielded her infant son from the sun by covering him with a blanket. Grace said, "Little Jackie was her life."

Vickie knew her dad as someone who, in addition to being highly intelligent, had an impeccable memory; this was affirmed during her phone conversation with Grace. Jack was correct in the belief that his mother's family did not like his father, and Jack was told by his dad that it was because Victoria's family was Catholic, and Smitty's family was Protestant. However, Grace claimed that she, her siblings, and their parents, didn't approve of Smitty as a husband. Grace referred to him as a "stinker" who took 10-year old Jackie away from Victoria and moved him in with one of Smitty's other women. Victoria searched for Jackie, even obtained a custody order for him, but she couldn't locate him, and she became so despondent, she killed herself. Victoria's family also accused Smitty of showing up at Victoria's funeral and stealing the money needed to pay for her burial.

In all the historical documents and during the phone conversation with Grace, Vickie realized that there was never any mention of Victoria having a mental illness or having been placed in mental hospital prior to her death. The coroner's report did, however, state that she was at her parents' home the night before she died. She was upset at not being able to find a job to get the money she needed to search for her son, so the doctor came to her parents' house and gave her shot to calm her nerves so she could sleep.

The next morning, Victoria came out of her bedroom and talked to her dad at 9 A.M., and then returned to her room. Later, when Victoria's mom went into the bedroom to check on her daughter, Victoria was gone. The bedroom window was left open, so it was assumed that Victoria climbed out and left. She took her coat but left her purse.

By obtaining copies of the coroner's report, Victoria's death certificate, and newspaper coverage of her suicide, Jack and Vickie discovered previously unknown specifics about Victoria's death. The newspaper article detailed Victoria's last steps from the moment she walked into the Security Bank Building just after 9:30 A.M., to entering the elevator and asking the elevator operator to take her to the sixth floor. There, she got off the elevator and looked around, and then returned to the elevator and went back to the bottom floor. Once on the bottom, Victoria told the elevator operator, "I want to go clear to the top."

When Victoria got to the 14th floor, she exited the elevator and climbed a wide staircase to the top floor. She removed her coat and left it in a small room before climbing out of a window and onto the ledge of the building. Overlooking the busy street below, Victoria walked to the south side of the

Above left: Jack, elementary school age, at the river with his mother

Left and above right: Jack, elementary school age

building, climbed over a small barrier and sat on the ledge with her feet dangling 10 stories above the rooftop of the adjacent Mason Building.

Victoria's final moments on the building top were witnessed by five people in the dental office of Dr. Barr, located on the seventh floor of the Patterson building a block away. The dentist, his dental assistant and three dental patients were concerned when they saw Victoria sitting on the ledge but decided not to call the superintendent of the Security Bank Building when they noticed a man in the window beneath her dangling feet. The witnesses suspected the woman on the ledge and the man in the window below were working together. The doctor went back to work, and ten to fifteen minutes later, Victoria place her hands in prayer position and use her right foot to dive off the ledge. The dental patients screamed.

Ten stories below the top of the south side of the Security Bank Building, Victoria landed feet first on the top of the Mason Building; her body bounced and landed 15 feet away. Victoria was lifeless. Employees in the Mason Building reported the moment of impact as the building shaking as though an "...earthquake had hit."

For the first time in the forty-six years that followed his mother's suicide, Jack read the details of how it happened and what a public spectacle it was. Information about Victoria was provided to the news and the coroner by Victoria's sister, Blanche, and her father, George. From news captions stating, "Woman Leaps to Death From Bank Building" to "Worry is Blamed for Suicide Leap" along with photos of the bank building and detectives working the scene of the death, names of the entire family were listed. In addition to Victoria and Smitty, the other name listed, the son she was searching for and despondent over, was referred to as "the child" (similar to the coroner's report,) but he was also identified as Jack in one story and his nickname, Jackie, in another. Newspaper coverage spread from the city of Fresno to as far north as Sacramento, and that, combined with breaking news radio coverage, personal information about Victoria, her estranged husband, and her son, and their domestic troubles, were put on public display.

The coroner's report echoed much of what was in the newspaper articles, but it also confirmed Jack's feeling of his mother's family keeping him at a distance when he was a child. Victoria's sister, Blanche, told the coroner that Smitty took Jackie away from Victoria when they were living in Pomona, and many other stories about his marriage to her sister. Blanche also talked a lot about Victoria, and she repeated Victoria's name throughout the interview, but in the coroner's transcript of the interview, Jackie's name was never mentioned. Blanche, the woman whose home Jackie often played at with his cousins, never referred to her own nephew by name when talking to the coroner. Instead, she called him "the child," "the boy," and "it." During the interview, the coroner asked Blanche if Victoria's parents were willing to take her in. Blanche responded, "Willing to take her but not the child. She wanted to get the boy and she didn't know what to do."

Jack's journey to the past was not filled entirely with good news and joyous reconciliation, but it was not all bad news either. Many of the questions and mysteries of his childhood were answered, and Jack knew his mother's last few months, or even her final moments and the description of the despondent woman leaping to her death, did not defined her life. Jack was just a child the last time he saw his mother alive, but he believed he knew her true heart and her strength; no stories of weakness and despair told by her siblings or newspaper reporters could change that. Jack took all the new documents and the photos he had obtained, placed them into his Samsonite, and went on believing the best about his mother.

Little Jackie Smith Became…

CHAPTER ELEVEN
Forgiving

Any additional questions that arose from the family research became, for both Jack and Vickie, less of an insult and more of a challenging stone to overturn. And there were many questions that continued to surface. For example, Victoria's siblings kept Jack at arms-length when he was a child and again as an adult; his daughter, Vickie, was ultimately treated the same. After the first phone conversation between Vickie and Grace, a friendly one, a second phone call was made; it was not the same. During the second phone call, Grace rudely asked Vickie what she wanted. Before Vickie could answer the question, Grace said, "We have enough family."

To the contrary, Grace's daughter, Linda, welcomed Jack and Vickie with arms open wide. Linda apologized for her mom being so rude to Vickie. Linda understood Vickie's desire for information about the family because in the seventies she, too, attempted family research. Linda asked questions but got only a few answers; if she tried to dig too deep, she was shut down by her mom and other relatives.

Linda was only five years old when her grandparents died, but she was always told that her mom's dad, George Lazar, was a stern, controlling man, and her mom's mom, Rosa, was a kind and loving lady. Linda was three years old when her aunt, Victoria, died but was nineteen years old when she found out that Victoria committed suicide—during the visit Jack, his wife, Ann, and their son, Alan, visited Grace and Linda's Fresno home in 1966. After that visit, Linda asked about her Aunt Victoria periodically through the years, but her mom wouldn't say much. Other family members were also reluctant or unwilling to talk much about Victoria. Linda said to Vickie, "Your grandmother's life is vague."

Growing up, Linda knew her deceased aunt, Victoria, had a son, but knew nothing of him or his whereabouts until he showed up at their house in 1966. Linda also knew nothing about her cousin, Jackie, having lived in foster homes as a child. In fact, that detail wasn't mentioned anywhere. Within all the documents pertaining to Victoria's life and death, and the conversations with Victoria's family members, no one mentioned Jackie having lived in foster homes when Victoria was a single mother. In the coroner's report, Victoria's sister, Blanche, mentioned the welfare department helping Victoria when Jack was young, but that was it. When Vickie brought it up during a phone conversation with Grace, she said she didn't remember him living in foster homes, only going to childcare because her sister, Victoria, had to work. When Vickie informed Grace that Jack remembered living in foster homes while his mom was at work on weekdays and he only saw her on weekends, Grace said, "Oh, that's probably just something made up in a child's imagination."

Vickie knew that children often see the world differently than adults. After all, as a child, she thought birds suddenly appeared every time her dad was near, that stars fell down from the sky every time he walked by, and on the day that he was born, the angels got together and created a dream come true. Vickie also knew it was possible for trauma to cause a child to create stories. Maybe her dad made up stories of his mother singing along to *Blue Moon* when she took Jackie to the theatre, maybe he wasn't really taken care of by the social outcasts in San Francisco, maybe he didn't run away from a dairy-farm foster home and work two jobs while attending school at age fourteen.

While Vickie understood that imaginary stories may happen in some cases of childhood trauma, she knew it was not what happened in this case, and not with her dad. Vickie had no question her dad's memory was close to exact, and to the best of Vickie's knowledge, her dad had never lied in his life. If Grace was going to accuse a person of making up stories as a child and still believing them as an adult, Vickie had news for Grace — she picked the wrong man to make that accusation about.

Linda offered to help Vickie with the family research, so they started working together. Then, the following summer, shortly after Vickie graduated with a bachelor's degree, she and Linda arranged to meet in person for the first time. Jack knew his mother would want him to reconnect as well. Family was important to his mother, even when they didn't see eye-to-eye. In her adult life, no matter how often she left Fresno, Victoria always returned to her family. Jack decided he would return to his family, too, so he left his home in Oroville and made the 90-minute drive south to Sacramento. From there, he rode with Vickie and her three daughters on the three-hour drive to Fresno. They met Linda and her

Jack with his granddaughters as he prepared to reunite with his mother's family, Fresno, Calif., 1997

Jack visiting his mother's grave, 1997

husband, Steve, at the cemetery in Fresno where Victoria was buried near her parents. Linda greeted Jack by telling him how much he looked like a member of the Lazar family.

After placing flowers on the graves, they went for lunch at a local restaurant. Surprisingly, Linda had convinced her mother, Grace, and another of Victoria's sisters, Camille, to join them. Linda was excited to see the physical family resemblance in Jack, and Vickie could see her own resemblance to her grandmother's sisters — they all had the same green eyes. Grace and Camille didn't talk much, but the others filled in any silence. After lunch, Camille invited everyone to her home for lemonade. Vickie and Linda didn't get much more family history out of Grace and Camille, but everyone was cordial, and it was a successful day in that regard. There were no offers from Grace or Camille to remain in touch with Jack or Vickie, but the relationship between Vickie and Linda had grown even stronger. Jack knew his mother would probably have been disappointed at her sisters' behavior, but not surprised, yet she would be thrilled at the family connections made between Jack, Vickie and Linda.

A month after the reunion of Jack with his aunts and meeting their cousin in Fresno, Vickie felt like she had reached a dead end in research about her grandmother and her family, but she told her dad about a story she read in her local newspaper about twins who were reunited after forty years apart. Prior to the family luncheon in Fresno, Jack had been separated from most of his mother's family for forty-seven years, and he hadn't seen Grace and Linda for thirty years. Vickie wondered if a newspaper reporter might find interest

Right: Jack looking at old photos with his cousin, Linda, 1997

Left: Jack with Vickie after reuniting with his mother's family, 1997

in the story of her dad reuniting with his family after so many years.

Vickie was also hoping she could use newspaper coverage to get additional information about her grandmother—just like when her dad used the media to get tips from the public regarding an investigation he was conducting. Vickie thought newspaper coverage might get her in touch with people who knew her grandmother, or maybe someone who knew more about her grandmother's state of mind before she died. If any of the witnesses to her grandmother's suicide were still alive, Vickie knew they likely would not have forgotten it. She was hopeful there were people out there who could fill in the gaps, and she hoped the media could help her reach them. Linda was supportive of the idea, and Jack was as well, because after all, Jack once told his daughter about investigative work, "Sometimes you have to act out of conventional or methodical means, and it seems it's then that things tend to fall in place."

On November 3, 1997, several months after initial contact was made with a reporter, Guy Keeler, at the *Fresno Bee* newspaper, a story was published. The reporter, however, didn't mention the reunion luncheon between Jack and his aunts. Instead, he focused the content of his story solely on Vickie's search for information about her grandmother. The story took up most of the entire front page of the *Fresno Bee*'s Life Section and most of the third page as well. The cover page displayed a large photo of Vickie, a smaller portrait photo of Victoria alone, and another of Little Jackie sitting on his mother's lap. Two pictures of the *Fresno Bee* suicide coverage from nearly forty-eight years earlier were also included. The story continued to the third page where among the text was a picture of Jack and Vickie taken earlier that year. Vickie was identified as Vickie Smith Foston, and Jack was either referred to by name, Jack Smith, or at times "Foston's father." The story was titled, "Granddaughter Asks Why?"

Vickie was a little bothered at the story not mentioning the reunion luncheon, but it didn't dampen her excitement over what the story did include. She was elated at the way the reporter told the story of her grandmother and her search for answers. Jack was thrilled as well. He told Vickie she shouldn't worry that it wasn't exactly what she planned; he told her he was proud of her, that she had done a great job, and together they would see where it went next. Like Jack and Vickie, Linda was happy with the outcome of the story; however, she did have to deal with the backlash from the Fresno family, including her mother and her aunts. Linda received several phone calls from relatives who were not particularly happy about their family business appearing in their hometown newspaper. One person asked Linda, "What is Vickie trying to prove?"

Vickie's post office box address was included in the story for anyone who wanted to share information about her grandmother, and over the next several days and weeks, letters rolled in. That led to follow-up phone calls with Victoria's friends, cousins and others, and within days, the picture of Victoria's life and death became much more complete, Jack's childhood finally began to make more sense, but the lives of many people in Jack's family would also take an unexpected turn.

Victoria's high school friend wrote Vickie a letter telling of what a nice person Victoria was, even as a teenager, and one of Smitty's distant family member confirmed the story of Victoria's suicide being associated with her not being able to find her son. That information was not a surprise to Jack and Vickie, but Victoria's first cousin, Mayo Goliti, did have surprising information to share. Mayo was an elderly man who grew up with Victoria and her siblings, and he said Victoria was the nicest of all the sisters. He talked to Vickie about how bad Victoria had it in her family, and how she was often mistreated by her older sisters. Mayo recalled a time when Victoria's sisters held her down to cut her hair. Mayo also told Vickie he thought it was great that she was asking questions, but he let her know that she wouldn't get any information out of Victoria's sisters. He said, "You're not going to get anything out of those girls. They've been lying their entire lives."

Mayo went on to disclose a deep Lazar family secret. Victoria's parents were not simply French and Italian as everyone claimed. Her mother, Rosa, was part Italian, but she was also half Armenian; Victoria's father was also Armenian. Victoria's parents, George and Rosa, were not Catholic as Jack always believed; they were Armenian Orthodox, and they were married in an Armenian Orthodox church in Fresno in 1901, shortly after they immigrated with their families from ancient Armenia (in eastern Turkey).

In the first half of the 20th century, like so many Armenian immigrants at the time, Victoria's parents settled in Fresno, California. Because of the massive influx of Armenians to the area, Armenians were discriminated against in Fresno, and Victoria's father, a businessman who spoke seven languages (including French), found it more profitable to conduct business as a Frenchman rather than as an Armenian. He removed the Armenian-identifying "ian" from his last name Lazarian and shortened it to a more French-sounding Lazar. Rosa spoke only Armenian, so she was kept away from

George's business dealings, and when asked, he identified her only as Italian.

Victoria and her siblings were raised at the nurturing hands of their mother, they learned the Armenian language, and they spent time with their Armenian grandparents, aunts, uncles, and cousins. However, as the Lazar children grew older, they, like their father, were determined to blend into life outside of the Armenian community. They adopted their father's false identity and distanced themselves from their cousin, Mayo, and other relatives who proudly identified as Armenian—even going so far as sometimes ignoring them in public. When Victoria's siblings got married (to non-Armenians), they continued to hide their true ethnic identity—some telling their children they only had Armenian relatives because Armenians married into their family.

Vickie was not familiar with the background or culture of the Armenian people, but Jack was. In his younger years, Jack spent several years in college and in his middle-age, he worked and traveled to various countries around the world. In fact, when Jack was working in Moscow and witnessed the gradual collapse of the Soviet Union after the failed coup attempt, Armenia was one of the republics to declare independence (after nearly seventy years under Soviet control). Once Jack settled back in Oroville, he was in his mid-fifties, and he furthered his education by spending time at the library checking out books on whatever topics interested him at the time.

Through years of continued education and exposure to cultures around the world, Jack knew the people of Armenia could be traced back thousands of years to the lands around Mt. Ararat and ancient Mesopotamia. He knew Armenia was once a vast kingdom, but that present-day Armenia was much smaller and landlocked with Turkey on the west, Georgia in the north, Azerbaijan on the east, and Iran to the south. Jack was also aware of the history of the Armenian people such as the roots of the Christian church and St. Gregory the Illuminator, the person credited with converting the nation of Armenia to Christianity in 301 AD, eleven years before the Romans.

Jack was familiar with the Armenian Genocide — the systematic mass killing of Armenians during World War I — a slaughter orchestrated by the Turkish government when at least 1.5 million Armenians were massacred in a short period of time. Jack knew that although the death toll was high during the Armenian Genocide, thousands of Armenian lives were saved with the help of brave Armenian revolutionaries who formed volunteer brigades to fight against Turkish aggression.

In discussions with Victoria's cousin, Mayo, Vickie brought up the topic of mental illness in the family. Mayo indicated that to some in the family, Victoria's declining mental state was not a complete surprise. Before Victoria was born, two of her mother's sisters were placed in mental institutions as young women, and each stayed there for the remainder of their lives. Several years after Victoria's death, Mayo's sister was treated with valium for depression, but, sadly, it only worsened her condition, and a short time later she stood in a field and died after setting herself on fire. Mayo himself was once treated for depression, and valium also made him suicidal, so he immediately stopped taking it. Mayo's insight into various family members battle with mental illness brought to question the shot given to Victoria to calm her nerves the night before her death and how much it may have contributed to her suicide.

Throughout the 18 months Vickie spent digging up his past, Jack handled everything with grace and dignity. The only known time he seemed to suffer PTSD from his childhood was several years after the death of a baby boy he tried to save when he was a detective; if Jack had any remaining triggers to his trauma, it wasn't obvious. He read every detail of his mother's death certificate, newspaper coverage of his mother's death, the cause of his mother's death, his father's involvement, and his family's admittance in the coroner's report to not helping to care for him when he was a child. Still, Jack didn't harbor anger or resentment. Jack believed his mother dealt with something no one else was able to understand, he believed Smitty thought he was being a protective father by keeping Jack from his mother, and he believed his mother's family probably had a reason for their behavior that they considered justified.

Ultimately, other than a tone of irritation in his voice when telling the story of the dairy farm foster parents trying to use him as a child laborer, Jack never said a mean-spirited word about anyone. Even when Vickie told Jack that Grace accused him of creating the story (in a child's imagination) about living in a foster home when his mom was alive, Jack didn't even attempt to defend himself — he just laughed. And there were other times Jack couldn't help but laugh while things unfolded, like the time Vickie was unable to locate Victoria and Smitty's marriage certificate. Jack jokingly told his daughter, "I might have to apologize to all the people who ever called me a bastard." Ultimately, that wasn't necessary because the marriage certificate was found.

Despite Jack's good-natured approach to his past unraveling, there were, however, times when the discussion was serious in nature, such as the time Vickie couldn't help but think of one detail in particular about Victoria's suicide; that she landed on her feet. Maybe she wasn't trying to kill herself, just trying to draw attention to her despair, or maybe she changed her mind or came to her senses during the fall — but to Vickie, Victoria landing on her feet seemed like an attempt at survival. Jack, Vickie and Linda also thought it was sad that so many members of Victoria's family lived so much of their lives in fear of being exposed. Grace went to the trouble of altering her birth certificate because it reflected the fact that she was born with an Armenian first and last name. And the lie was a hard one to let go of. When Linda confronted family members with the truth, Victoria's siblings denied knowing they were Armenian and even questioned the accuracy of the research. There were others, however, like Linda's sister, Sandi, and younger generations who accepted and celebrated the news.

Linda and Vickie began referring to each other as, "My Armenian Cousin," and both were happy to share their newfound ancestry with anyone they knew. Jack was just as thrilled. Jack had embraced diversity as a child when he lived in what he called the "mixed bag" of foster children at Mrs. Black's home, in middle school when he lived among the social outcasts in San Francisco, through his teens when making friends and playing sports in school, and as a law enforcement officer he enjoyed patrolling and getting to know the people in diverse communities within Butte County. Later in life, one of the reasons Jack accepted work assignments in remote areas of Alaska and overseas was to learn more about cultures different than his own. Throughout Jack's life, he developed close friendships with people of various races and ethnicities, discovered traditions within other cultures, learned to respect values different from his own, understood religious differences, shared a variety of foods, and better understood the struggles of other races and cultures — sometimes even supporting the battles his friends and loved ones fought.

In addition to his friendships and working environment, by the nineties, Jack's personal life had grown more diverse as well; Alan's wife was Filipino, Vickie's husband was Black and Japanese, and Jack's granddaughters were multiracial. Jack loved his family and every cultural background it represented, and he welcomed the news about his own newfound Armenian ancestry. In fact, the day after the news of his Armenian heritage was discovered, Jack proudly told a friend, "Yesterday morning I woke up French and Italian, and at night I went to bed Armenian!"

Another contact Vickie made from the "Granddaughter Asks Why?" newspaper article helped even more in putting the pieces of the puzzle together. After reading the *Fresno Bee* newspaper on November 3, two sisters, Lena and Lydia, both in their early seventies, were anxious to talk to Vickie. Lena wrote to Vickie about seeing the newspaper article early that morning and was surprised to see a picture of a little boy she once knew. Lena immediately called her sister, Lydia, and told her to get up and get her paper because, "Little Jackie Smith is on the front page of the Life Section."

Lena and Lydia, Armenians whose maiden name was Avedikian, told Vickie the picture in the newspaper of Jackie sitting on Victoria's lap was taken in the front yard of their childhood home; their dad took the picture. After seeing Little Jackie in the "Granddaughter Asks Why?" article, Lydia said she looked through old pictures all day and cried. Lena told Vickie, "Your father was our foster brother when he was a little boy."

Jack and Vickie thought the time they met Linda at the cemetery, put flowers on Victoria's grave, and had lunch with Victoria's sister's Grace and Camille in 1997 would be the last trip to Fresno for quite some time. However, Lena and Lydia asked if they could see their former foster brother, so in 1998, Jack and Vickie returned to Fresno, this time to reunite with former foster siblings; Linda joined them, as did Lena and Lydia's family and friends. Lena, Lydia, their other sister, Lucy, their brother, Kerry (and their spouses) were welcoming and loving; they showed everyone pictures and, unlike the response from Victoria's siblings, they wanted to talk about the past. Also, unlike the response Jack got from his mother's siblings, Lena was the first to say, "I always wondered what became of Little Jackie."

Jack with the Avedikian foster siblings, 1998

Little Jackie's foster family asked him about his life after his mother's death. Jack talked briefly about his time in law enforcement and about working overseas while Vickie sat back quietly thinking of her own answer to their question. Outside of thinking of her dad as a small-town lawman, like Andy Taylor of Mayberry, with an adventurous life, Vickie could describe her dad as a man of faith, a man of integrity, a man who, no matter what, always tried to do the right thing and who refused to compromise his principles. The Little Jackie known by the Avedikians grew up to become a walking example of unconditional love. If Vickie were to have answered the question briefly, she would have described her dad has having become the most wonderful man in the world who comforted everyone he met and whose smile lit up a room.

Lena and Lydia talked about Victoria, complimented how she always kept herself up so nicely, and no matter where she was working over the years, a café, a motel, a Chinese Food restaurant, a liquor store, or Long's Drug Store, she always made time for Jackie on the weekends. Lena and Lydia shared stories of how they waited on their front porch with Jackie on Saturday mornings, and he would get excited whenever he saw his mom walking up the street from the bus stop. He would jump up and down and yell, "Here comes my bus, Mommy, here comes my bus, Mommy." Lena, a young teenager at the time, said she was happy to see Jack with his mother, but when Victoria took him for the day, or for the weekend, Lena had a fear that Victoria would not bring him back.

Just two doors down the street from Lena's home, Lydia was still living in the same home she and Lena grew up in, and where Little Jackie lived with their family, so Jack was invited to walk through it. Jack had vivid memories of the layout of the inside of their home, sleeping in a crib in one of the bedrooms, running his own bath for the first time, peaking down a manhole cover in a nearby alley, and an image of their father chopping heads off of chickens in the backyard. He didn't, however, remember that they were Armenian. In fact, Jack recalled his foster mother speaking to him in a foreign language, but for some reason he grew up thinking it had been Portuguese. Before leaving Lydia's house, Jack posed for a picture on the same front porch he waited so excitedly for his "bus mommy."

Jack didn't remember why he had to move from the Avedikian house to Mrs. Black's home, so Lena and Lydia explained that their mother had become ill and wasn't able to take care of him. Jack told Lena and Lydia he remembered, after being moved to Mrs. Black's foster home, returning to their home for a birthday party. Lena and Lydia confirmed Jack's memory. They told Jack that their dad used to pick him up from Mrs. Black's and bring him back to their home for birthday parties, or to visit, and when he had to take Jackie home, their dad would drop Jackie off at his new home, and then sit in his car and cry.

Lydia was in college when she heard about Victoria's suicide. The newspaper reported that Jackie was living with his father in Los Angeles, so Lydia took a break from school, traveled to Los Angeles, and, to no avail, tried to find Jackie. Lena and Lydia said they thought about Jackie a lot over the years, even talked about him to their spouses and their children. As they looked through photos of Jackie as a child, Jack whispered to Vickie and asked if she brought the pictures with her. Vickie whispered back and said, "No Dad, they saved these."

One thing Jack and Vickie learned from the Avedikian sisters was that Victoria didn't go to great lengths to hide her Armenian identity. When she first took her toddler son to foster services, she disclosed her Armenian heritage to them, so she was assigned an Armenian social service worker, and that person placed Jack in an Armenian foster home—the Avedikians' home. Knowing this, Jack and Vickie suspected

Victoria's family allowed Jack to live in foster care instead of taking him into their own homes because they thought Jack knew he was Armenian, and they feared he might say something to his cousins; their secret was safer the further away Little Jackie stayed. Also, Jack and Vickie believed Victoria was treated differently by her family because she didn't live the same lie they lived, and their lack of support when she needed to find her son may not have been why she wanted to die, but it may have contributed to the reason she chose such a public suicide — Victoria may have wanted to draw attention to her family and expose the lie that caused such division among them. Her public suicide didn't, however, draw much attention to her family because it was her sister, Blanche, who gave the police, the media, and the coroner only the narrative of Victoria's troubled marriage, and she protected exposure of the family lie — for the time being.

The "Granddaughter Asks Why?" article took Jack on another adventure, one in which he was not the only person sharing memories of Victoria — but others who confirmed the strong, loving woman he adored as a child; an adoration that continued throughout his life. Jack added childhood photos given to him by Lena and Lydia, and the "Granddaughter Asks Why?" newspaper article to his Samsonite — the first-time pictures of Jack, his mother, and his daughter were all displayed together.

Little Jackie Smith Became...

CHAPTER TWELVE
A Loving Grandfather

During the mid-1990s, Jack began to focus on his physical health. He started eating organic foods, lots of grains and vegetables and less meat — with only a few snacks in between. Jack tried to cut back on smoking cigarettes, but a habit that started when he was a teenager was too hard to stop completely. Jack moved out of the apartment he shared with Tony and into a home of his own where he assembled a fitness corner with physical therapy band and hand weights. Jack worked out nightly.

In addition to physical health, Jack continued to maintain his mental health. Still working post-retirement, he had given up hauling heavy items and instead chose lighter-weight deliveries. Working as a part-time night courier, he collected and delivered bank receipts, giving him the opportunity for nightly, peaceful, scenic drives through the mountain roads, orchards, and farms he once patrolled as a deputy — without the daytime traffic. For his spiritual health, Jack kept a Bible on the desk in his new home for easy reference, said his nightly prayers, hung a poem titled "A Creed to Live By," and posted a small piece of paper on his refrigerator which read, "this too shall pass" as a reminder when times were challenging.

Jack turned sixty years old in the late 1990s, and he was no longer interested in romance or the dating scene. He mentioned to Alan how he enjoyed the trips he used to make to Reno for gambling and the nice legs of the cocktail waitresses, but he wasn't pursuing women — Jack didn't feel a need for a relationship. He laughed, however, when he told Vickie that in the 1970s, the young waitresses at the diner offered to introduce him to their friends, and in the 1980s and 1990s, they wanted to introduce him to their mothers. After the turn of the century, Jack said the opportunities were still presented to him, but at this point, the young waitresses at the diner wanted to introduce him to their grandmothers. Jack laughed when he told Vickie he thanked the waitresses and respectfully declined.

Though Jack wasn't interested in a relationship for himself, he was happy and supportive for those who did. Alan and Vickie had both divorced their first spouses in the late 1990s; when they chose to remarry in the early 2000s, Jack was there to celebrate. And when Jack gave his daughter away a second time, it happened to be to an Armenian man, Glen Odabashian. The wedding was officiated by Vickie's evangelical pastor, Jonathan Zachariou, and the priest of the Sacramento Armenian Apostolic Church, Father Yeghia Hairabedian — both of whom were family friends. Jack was also supportive when Tony, his long-time friend and former roommate, married again, and was thrilled to attend the wedding of his former stepdaughter, Lori, to which he took Vickie along as his plus-one. Jack also enjoyed some of India's cultural traditions when the daughter of his close friend (a local businessman) was married.

In preparation for a wedding, Jack constructed a poem that

expressed his feelings about marriage, and exposed his spiritual and romantic sides. Jack wrote that a wedding was a celebrated event directed by the laws and hand of man to pledge unity; that marriage was the sustenance of unity guided by the laws and hand of God; and for the union he added, "May the illuminating canopy of enduring grace guide and protect you; may your hearts be filled with harmony and joy immersed in the tender warmth of everlasting love. God Bless."

Despite Jack's lack of personal interest in romance, there was one woman whose flirtatious nature Jack could not resist (mostly because he knew it was innocent and done in jest). In 1990, when Vickie and her first husband, Dean, moved into their first home, they chose a center house on a small block of three houses. In the home on one side, a young girl, Lia, lived with her family. Lia became an occasional childcare provider of Dean and Vickie's daughters. Over the years, Lia remained a close family friend who Vickie began to refer to as "My Peruvian daughter". The neighbor on the other side of Dean and Vickie's house was an elderly woman named Lily. She was eighty years old, and widowed, when Dean and Vickie first moved in, and over the years, Lily became a close family friend who attended many of the parties and holiday celebrations held at Dean and Vickie's home. During that time, Lily flirted with any nice-looking man she saw — and Jack was no exception. In fact, because of his shy nature, over the years, Jack was one of Lily's favorite targets. Even though Lily was old enough to be Jack's mother (Lily was born in 1911, four years before Victoria was born) Jack laughed along with family and friends whenever Lily made flirtatious comments to, or about, him. In 2002, at Vickie and Glen's wedding, Lily's light-natured flirtation was obvious to the wedding photographer, so a photo was staged in which Lily was caught flirting with Jack. Lily, aged ninety-two at the time, decided she would blow into Jack's ear. Jack complied, and the image of a was caught on camera.

When Jack wasn't working as a night courier, he maintained a regular schedule in his personal life. Every day of the week, at noon and at 5 P.M., Jack met with his friends at his favorite diner, Cornucopia — located in the same building as his favorite diner in the 1970s, and part of the 1980s and 1990s, only the name of the diner changed over the years. And like in years past, each time Jack entered the diner he was greeted by diner staff and a few customers (again, like Norm on *Cheers*, just not in unison). He replied with a smile and said "Howdy" before taking his usual seat at the counter next to three or four of his coffee buddies.

Later each evening, Jack returned to the diner so he could be alone with a laptop and he would research the internet for any topic he had interest in at the time. While at the diner, Jack often ran into old friends and family, like his former roommate, Tony, or his second wife, Patricia, her daughter, Lori, and Patricia's elderly mother, Pearl, so he would join them at their table to catch up on life. Occasionally, outside of the diner, Jack would accept a dinner invitation at the homes of his friends, Roger and Dena, and his friend and former colleague at the sheriff's department, Mary Jane Perrucci.

Another of Jack's favorite pastimes was playing the penny

Jack with Vickie and Glen, and their children, 2001 Christmas card

Jack with Lily at Vickie and Glen's wedding, 2002 (Photo courtesy of Sandreia Vianna)

Jack with Vickie at her wedding, 2002 (Photo courtesy of Sandreia Vianna)

slots at the local Indian casino—he liked to play Caveman Keno. Jack's spending limit during this time was a conservative maximum loss of $5, but the amount was only that small because of one of the few areas in which Jack seemed to lose some self-control—gambling (it had been one of Smitty's weaknesses as well). Jack had experienced a few bouts of gambling losses in his adult life, but in the late 1990s, he finally learned his lesson. At the time, Jack was sharing a house with his friend, Tony, and he hoped for riches in Las Vegas. He lost money there, went back to Oroville, then he went to Reno to give gambling a second shot. A day or so later, Jack called Tony to tell him his card-table winnings were up to $30k. Tony suggested Jack quit right then and come home, but Jack didn't take his friend's advice, and he returned home a day later with no money. From that point on, for the most part, Jack limited his gambling deposit to $5 per visit and only on penny slot machines.

In December 1999, Jack attended Vickie's graduation ceremony; she earned a master's degree in sociology. Apparently, while Vickie was in school, she developed an interest in writing, because one year later, Jack was reading a manuscript his daughter wrote about his mother's life, the research he and Vickie conducted, and the discoveries made. Jack was excited about his daughter's new endeavor and offered feedback and support in any way he could.

Vickie began her grandmother's biography with a childhood image she created of watching someone she believed to be her grandmother; a woman standing at the top of a building in a small, western-style town. Watching her,

Vickie tried to find a facial expression or some indication of what the woman was feeling, but Vickie was never able to clearly see her face. In the image, the woman never jumped – she just stood there, as if in contemplation, with her hair and clothes flowing in the breeze. Vickie wrote that she carried the image of her grandmother into adulthood, but she never told anyone about it – including her dad. Jack first learned of this childhood image his daughter created about his mom when he proofread her manuscript.

Vickie went on to write about the steps she took in obtaining information about her grandmother – the class assignment that prompted the search, phone calls with her dad, one-on-one meetings with her dad at his favorite diner, her dad's involvement in research of historical documents, reaching out to the media, contact with Victoria's siblings, and cousinships developed with her grandmother's extended Armenian family members Linda, Susie, and Annette. Vickie included family photos, maps, her own words, and quotes by others in the book.

Several chapters into the manuscript, Vickie changed her writing from first-person narrative to creative non-fiction where Vickie wrote in first-person as if she was her grandmother telling her own childhood stories, her family history, and the establishment of the French and Italian false identity started by her father and continued within her generation. In addressing the Armenian Genocide, true accounts of victims who escaped the slaughter ordered by the Turkish Government (which were previously written in other forms of literature) were included as though they were stories

Victoria was personally exposed to through her fictional Armenian neighbors. In the biography, the names of Victoria's family members were changed. Instead of using their real names, Vickie replaced three of her grandmother's sisters' names with those belonging to some of Vickie's long-term girlfriends: Ellen, Veronica, and Angelique.

Based on what Vickie had been told about her grandmother's character, when she wrote in first-person as Victoria, Vickie chose to have her grandmother behave like Jack; she believed the two were very much alike. With Vickie's own experience as a mother and a wife, she tried her best to create the emotions she believed her grandmother may have felt during various circumstances, while responding to them the way she believed her dad would. In writing her grandmother's story, Vickie researched slang used from the 1920s through the 1940s, and as part of the creative non-fiction, she blended separate situations together to simplify the story, sometimes creating dialogue to help describe a scene, and Vickie also threw a bit of her own personal experience into her grandmother's life as well.

In the final chapters of the manuscript, Vickie returned to first-person writing as herself, but her words were specifically directed to her grandmother; everything revealed by the research and how it changed her dad's life and the lives of so many others, how they established relationships with younger generations of their blood-relatives, as well as the foster sisters, Lena and Lydia, and in addition to discovering they were Armenian, how they also found out the small Italian portion of their bloodline was specific to Sicily.

Each chapter of the biography was titled after a song Vickie thought was appropriate for the content within the chapter – songs she listened to and was emotionally inspired by when writing; musical artists like Celine Dion, Heart, Steve Perry, Theresa, and Natalie Grant to name a few. Of course, because Vickie was writing Victoria's story, one of the chapters was also titled after the song *Blue Moon*. Vickie titled her body of work *Victoria's Secret: A Conspiracy of Silence*, and despite the name sounding familiar, the book contained no similarities to the lingerie store, but was the most appropriate title out of each one Vickie considered. Vickie dedicated the book to her dad, whom she called, "…my hero."

When the manuscript was complete, proofread by several friends, and edited by a friend who taught an English Literature class at a local university, Vickie decided on an attempt at self-publishing; six months later, boxes of books were delivered to her doorstep. Vickie's work schedule was too busy for her to drive to Oroville right away, so she immediately mailed a copy of the book to her dad. Less than a week later, Vickie and her daughters drove to meet Jack at his favorite diner, Cornucopia. When they pulled into the parking lot, Jack was standing in front of the restaurant waiting for them, as he usually did. After parking, Vickie and her daughters were walking toward Jack when Vickie noticed the envelope in which she mailed the book to her dad was clutched beneath his arm. Vickie looked at her dad's face, and he was smiling so brightly, for a moment she didn't see the man she always knew, rather, he had the face of a happy little boy — Little Jackie was standing there. Vickie looked down at the ground so her dad couldn't see her eyes well with tears, and when she looked back up, he was a man again — but still with a huge smile on his face.

Inside the diner, the experience was much like it had always been since Vickie's childhood. They entered the diner, and Jack was greeted aloud by several people. When they were seated in a booth, people walking by stopped to talk to her dad — some were old enough to possibly be the same diner patrons who visited their booth when Vickie was a child. This time, however, after Jack introduced the visitors to his daughter and granddaughters, he pulled the book out of the envelope and boasted about it. In the years prior, he was thrilled to announce to his friends that his daughter, a woman, was the first in his family to obtain a bachelor's degree, then she went even further and earned a master's degree, and on that day he proudly displayed her accomplishment as a published author of a book about his mother, another strong woman he loved and respected dearly. Jack never bragged about anything that he was directly involved in, and as a subject of the book, one of the researchers, and father of the author, he must have been so thrilled about the roles his mother and daughter played, he forgot about his own involvement.

Less than a month later, Jack received a phone call from Vickie. She had been in Los Angeles for book signings at two Armenian bookstores and had been interviewed on Armenian television. Vickie was excited to tell her dad that when she and her daughters were driving home to Sacramento from Los Angeles, they happened to go to the top of the Security

"Victoria's Secret" book cover

Bank Building with the building owner and television news crews. Vickie was going to be interviewed at the top of the building about her book the following week.

Jack continued to receive phone calls from Vickie as she traveled for book signings, radio and television interviews, and speaking engagements, most of which were Armenian-owned venues or Armenian-sponsored events. Never one to be the center of attention, Jack was happy to know Vickie was sharing stories about his mother and of his childhood, and he was content to sit back and live vicariously through her experience.

In September 2001, a few months after Vickie's book was published, she scheduled a book signing in Oroville. Prior to the book signing, a book review was included in the *Oroville Mercury* newspaper, and the local Oroville connection was made when Jack's background as an investigator with the Butte County Sheriff's Department was mentioned. Jack's name had been mentioned numerous times in the *Oroville Mercury* newspaper over the years, as a graduating high school senior in 1957, as the father of a newborn daughter in 1967, and as a deputy and investigator throughout most of the seventies, and in review of his daughter's book in 2001, he happily accepted being referred to as "the author's father."

Much like the concern first voiced by Lena, one of the foster sisters Jack reunited with in 1998, during Vickie's speaking engagements for her grandmother's biography, mostly from 2001 through 2003, people often asked her "What was your dad's life like after his mother's suicide?" and "What did your dad make of his life?" Vickie's answer was usually brief. She told them that he overcame a lot of obstacles, worked in law enforcement, and was the most amazing man she had ever known. Armenians often attributed his resilience to his Armenian bloodline.

Because there were so many requests for more information about what became of Victoria's son, Vickie knew there was much more that could be told about her dad – and she wanted to be the one to write it. Vickie asked her dad if she could write his biography next, and Jack was all in. So, just as they had in preparation for Victoria's life story, Jack and Vickie talked during family get togethers at her house in Sacramento, and during breaks from work on holidays and summer vacation. On numerous occasions, in Oroville, Vickie met Jack at a diner where they found a booth or table in a quiet place (to keep the number of interruptions to a minimum) and would have breakfast or lunch in the diner while Vickie interviewed Jack, then they would take a break for what Vickie called "father-daughter bonding time" on the slot machines at the Indian casino. Afterwards, they often returned to the diner for more discussion, and more food.

As Jack told his daughter detailed stories about his life, he slowly pulled items of remembrance from his piece of vintage Samsonite luggage; this included a newspaper clipping of Ronald Reagan from the dedication of the Oroville Dam, the *Master Detective Magazine* in which Jack was featured, the Yuba City newspaper story of when Jack was the victim of a convenience store robbery, the media photo of the *Ramona R.* sinking off the coast of Ft. Bragg, letters of commendation, pictures and VHS videos of Alaska and Moscow, and magazines with stories of the Belgrade demonstrations. Also in Jack's Samsonite were the items Vickie had given him; the 1950 *Fresno Bee* coverage of his mother's suicide, the 1997 *Fresno Bee* newspaper article, "Granddaughter Asks Why?", the book Vickie wrote about his mother, and the numerous news accounts from Vickie's book tours.

If at any time the Samsonite didn't provide Jack with enough remembrance of his involvement in yesterday's news, television and radio helped trigger memories. By the 2000s, true-crime documentary television shows like *48 Hours* and *Dateline* had replaced the *Master Detective* magazines of the 1970s and 1980s — prompting memories of Jack's experience in law enforcement. Jack was also reminded of his time as a deputy when he was interviewed by a local Oroville writer who contributed scripts to some of the crime-drama television shows; she intertwined some of his experiences into her storyline.

In local news, former Butte County Deputy, Perry Reniff, was elected Butte County Sheriff-Coroner in 2002. Reniff was new to the sheriff's department in 1972 when Jack was a detective, and between that time and Jack's retirement from the sheriff's department in 1976, Reniff worked on numerous cases with Jack. Reniff was one of the first officers to arrive on the scene in what became Jack's successfully solved case "Riddle of the Hogtied Nude in the Creek", and he worked alongside Jack for the rescue of Ron Wood and the dog in the snow-covered mountains, and for the recovery of the airman's body from the bottom of Feather Falls. In 2007, Sheriff Reniff was pictured on CBS news assisting a family who had been rescued from being stranded for three days in the snow-covered mountains north of Paradise. The incident was reminiscent of Jack's time as a member of the Butte County Search and Rescue Team, and just one of the many reminders of the highly qualified, skilled members he worked with in the department. The 2007 rescue led by Sheriff Reniff was considered by one of the responding paramedics as "nothing short of a miracle," and the following day, the family was interviewed by Anderson Cooper on CNN.

In 2011, Jack attended the funeral of Tom Butler, a former Butte County deputy and someone Jack respected and befriended during their time together in the sheriff's department. Tom Butler was one of the officers who responded, with Jack, to the domestic violence call of a man who shot himself in front of his daughter, and who Jack eventually talked into dropping his weapon in the middle of a field. Tom Butler was one of the officers who commended Jack for his bravery during the incident. Shortly after Tom Butler's funeral, Jack started attending the Butte County Sheriff's Department "old-timers" luncheons where he reconnected with some of the men and women with whom he proudly served the community thirty-plus years earlier.

Also in 2011, reminders of the 1997 discovery of his Armenian heritage surfaced when word spread around Chico and Oroville that a memorial had been built to honor a famous Armenian, General Andranik Ozanian. In the late 19th and early 20th centuries (including World War I and the Armenian Genocide), General Andranik (as he was known) successfully led volunteer revolutionary armies against Turkish military aggression — saving thousands of Armenians from being slaughtered. General Andranik also influenced heads of governments around the world to support an independent Armenia, and he was referred to as, "The Armenian's Robin Hood, Garibaldi, and Washington, all in one."

Residents of Butte County learned from local news that after World War I, General Andranik moved to the Armenian Diaspora community in Fresno (where Jack's grandparents were also living, and his mother was a toddler). General Andranik then moved to San Francisco, and apparently, in 1927, sought treatment for an illness at a hot springs resort at Richardson Springs in Northern California — located in Butte County, 32 miles northwest of Oroville. On August 31, 1927, General Antranik died at the hot springs. The cause of death was listed as angina. His passing was mourned around the world; monuments and statues were erected in his honor in major cities within the countries of Armenia, Romania, France, and Cyprus. However, a memorial was not built at the hot springs, the site of General Andranik's passing, until 2010, more than eighty years after his death, when a Christian organization, YWAM, which owned the hot springs, and a group of Northern California Armenians, erected a memorial near the entrance to the resort. A bubbling fountain made of local rock was built with a plaque that reads: *General Andranik Ozanian, hero of the Armenian people, died at the Springs August 31, 1927. This spring serves to remind us of the victims of persecution around the world, and specifically the 1,500,000 victims of the 1915-1918 genocide in Armenia.*

As Vickie typed away at her dad's life story, news stories in the 2000s helped give her a better understanding of some of her dad's life experiences from the 1960s through the 1990s. When Serbian president Slobodan Milosevic (who was also the Serbian President when Jack was in Yugoslavia) was put on trial in 2002 for war crimes (including genocide) in Kosovo,

General Andranik Ozanian's memorial, Richardson Springs Resort, Butte County, Calif.

Croatia, and Bosnia, Vickie realized the historical importance of the demonstrations her dad witnessed in Belgrade. When Ronald Reagan died in 2004, Vickie saw television footage of his time as California governor, images from a time in which she was too young to remember, but she could envision then-Governor Reagan walking up to her dad in a parking lot.

Also in 2004, Vickie watched the local news coverage of San Jose Bible College, the school for ministry that her dad had attended after he graduated from high school, and how it had relocated its campus from San Jose to Rocklin, a small town on the outskirts of Sacramento — not far, in fact, from the dairy-farm foster home her dad ran away from as a young teen. The college name had been changed to William Jessup University in honor of the founder, and the school president the year Jack attended. The number of students enrolled in the college had increased from 122 when Jack attended during the 1957-58 school year to more than 400 students when the campus moved to Rocklin.

While Vickie was researching her dad's life, she located the motel in which her dad lived in 1952 when he was a twelve-year old and was cared for by the social outcasts in the Tenderloin District of San Francisco. It just so happened, the second-story motel and the restaurant below it, Original Joe's, whose neon sign would light up Jack's room, were both still open for business, so Vickie, along with her three daughters and her husband, Glen, dined at the Original Joe's restaurant. After lunch, Vickie attempted to enter the motel her dad had lived in more than fifty years earlier; the entry door was at ground level and adjacent to Original Joe's entry, but unfortunately, she didn't feel it was safe to enter after seeing that the staircase leading to the motel rooms was cluttered with people, some of whom appeared to be homeless and were unconscious. Vickie took photos and later showed them to her dad. He smiled at the good memories the photos brought back. Unfortunately, a few years later, Original Joe's caught fire, and so too did several of the motel rooms above the restaurant. The fire damage to the restaurant, which originally opened in 1937, was so severe that the restaurant closed indefinitely in 2007.

In 2010, news footage of the Deepwater Horizon oil spill in the Gulf of Mexico provided images of how the ocean water

The motel Jack lived in when he was 12 years old, San Francisco Tenderloin District

must have appeared in the months following the 1989 Exxon Valdez oil spill in Alaska. Sadly, the Deepwater Horizon oil spill was even more destructive to humans, marine life, and the environment than the *Exxon Valdez* oil spill had been. Two years later, the release of the movie *Big Miracle* provided Vickie with images of the north slope of Alaska, a place her dad lived and worked for the better part of the 1980s. And in the movie, reference was made to Prudhoe Bay, the location of Jack's employer and the place from where a barge was sent to help rescue the whales trapped under the ice. Unfortunately, the ice was too thick and the barge from Prudhoe Bay couldn't break through, but the Russian government's ice breaker eventually did.

As excited as Jack was to walk through his past and tell his daughter as much about it as he could, and as much as he was looking forward to reading how she would pull it all together in written form, Jack also knew that writing his life story might take Vickie longer than she anticipated because his daughter's life had become much busier since she wrote and published his mother's biography. In addition to Vickie's day job at the school for at-risk youth and the classes she taught at least one night each week at local hospitals, marriage to her second husband expanded her immediate family; she added two young-adult stepsons to her own three daughters (and several other new extended family members). As a result, Vickie and her husband hosted more social gatherings and held more birthday and other celebratory parties than before, and their family traveled more as well. In addition, Vickie's three daughters entered their teens and their activities became much more time consuming than when her children were young.

Jack understood that Vickie's research and writing time was limited to available weekends, holidays, and summer vacations, and he was there for her when she had questions or needed information. As "the author's father," however, he wasn't only available for writing support; Jack was supportive of his daughter (and the rest of his family) whenever he was needed — and because Vickie's life had shown patterns similar to his with unexpected, unlikely, and even newsworthy events — there were a lot of moments for which Jack provided support that had nothing to do with Vickie's writing project.

For a man who grew up with several, temporary or part-time, long-term examples of what a father should be, Jack didn't just have the label of "Dad" given to him because he fathered children. Rather, it was because he filled the role lovingly. And for a man who had limited memories of his own grandparents and no real examples of what the role of a grandparent involved, he delighted in being "Grandpa Jack." Whenever he could, Jack drove from Oroville to Sacramento for his granddaughters' extra-curricular activities. One memorable activity Jack was able to attend in 2005 was a high school musical, *Grease*. Held at El Camino High School on a makeshift stage in the school cafeteria, Jack's oldest granddaughter, Courtney, was cast as the character Cha-Cha, and just after she and the character, Danny, won the Hand Jive competition, there was anticipation for his granddaughter's celebratory slow dance to the song *Blue Moon*. Sadly, the song wasn't played—the scene ended with the Hand Jive competition. Thankfully, however, if Jack was missing the song during those years, another remake of the original had recently been released by Rod Stewart in a collaboration with Eric Clapton.

Jack also drove to Sacramento for his granddaughters' high school graduations, birthday parties, and most of the holiday gatherings at Vickie's house—and because his birthday was only five days apart from his granddaughter, Moriah's, birthday, he never wanted to take the attention away from her, but at Moriah's request, he occasionally agreed to share a birthday party with her. Jack spent time watching his granddaughter's grow from playing on the trampoline in Vickie's backyard to each girl getting her own car and driving way. Jack was also thrilled to see his granddaughter's follow in some of his own footsteps: Courtney and Moriah were involved in Christian missionary work in their teens and, with the help of Jack's financial support, they traveled to help the needy in Fiji, France, Greece, and Brazil. Also, like Jack, his youngest granddaughter, Jordan, became an avid horseback rider.

Jack was proud to see his granddaughter's grow into strong, independent, and educated young women. He knew they would face obstacles in their lives, including gender and/or racial barriers they would likely have to fight at some point, but he knew they would always have the support of a loving family (including Jack), and he hoped they would never end up as despondent as his mother was the day she took her own life—unable to find a job, in part because she

Jack's birthday hike with Alan and Vickie, Echo Lake, Calif., 2001

was a woman, and lost without the support of her family. Jack believed the world offered more opportunities for women in the 2000s than it had for his mother, a woman whose financial independence was suppressed by the era and culture in which she lived, and that his granddaughter's would be successful as long as they took advantage of those opportunities. In return for the unconditional love and support their Grandpa Jack gave them, Courtney, Moriah, and Jordan adored him. It was obvious when their faces lit up whenever they were around him.

Jack enjoyed the family get-togethers at Vickie's house, in part so he could discuss engine modifications he made to his car with Vickie's second-husband, Glen, and Glen's sons, Aaron and Adam—an interest all four men had in common.

Jack on boat, Echo Lake, 2001

Though Alan and his second wife, Isela, made periodic visits to see Jack in Oroville, Jack also used time during events at Vickie's house to catch up on details of Alan's various business ventures. In addition, after Jack's first great-granddaughter, Kalli, was born in 2011, he was excited to see her, and he proudly kept her picture displayed in front of all other photos on his desk.

Regardless of the purpose of the gathering or celebration at Vickie's house, Jack always brought gifts: the grandchildren under age 18 received a card with cash inside, and always signed proudly with his signature closure, *All My Love, GP Jack*. Anyone over age 18 received a card from Jack with California Lottery Scratchers inside (and sometimes cash too), and again, with his signature closure, "All My Love" followed by either "Dad" or "Jack." Jack also brought pies from Cornucopia — the same diner in which he met with his friends for coffee twice each day and where he sat alone and conducted research on his laptop late in the evening. Cornucopia prepared an assortment of typical 24-hour diner foods but specialized in making pies; their motto was "The Pie Is Why."

Jack's family and friends loved the lottery scratchers and the pies so much, they began to look forward to potential big winnings from Jack's lottery scratchers (the highest of which occurred when Vickie's husband won $500 on Father's Day), and Vickie's friends placed special pie-orders ahead of Jack's visit. Jack turned 70 years old in 2009, and was only working part-time and drawing Social Security, but he was happy to provide something people found joy in. Believing just as he did as twelve-year-old living under the care of social outcasts in San Francisco with nothing to his name but the ability to rescue injured pigeons, Jack found something he could offer to others while living on a fixed, retirement income. Pies and lottery scratchers became Jack's way of giving back to his family, friends, and community simply for the love and support they gave him.

When the crowds died down at Vickie's house after a party or a holiday function, Jack would hang out, take a nap on the couch, wake up, eat leftovers and watch movies. Alan often stuck around as well. On one of those nights, the movie they chose to watch was *Forrest Gump*. Though Alan and Vickie had each seen the movie countless times, when they watched it that night with Jack, something dawned on Vickie – Forrest Gump was a small-town man who was unexpectedly featured in the headlines and who personally experienced numerous, high-profile historical events in his lifetime. At one point during the movie, Vickie looked at her dad, laughed, and said, "Oh my gosh, Dad, that's you!" Alan followed Vickie's exclamation with a chuckle and said, "Yep!" Jack didn't say a word, he just laughed.

For Alan and Vickie, nothing could replace the similarities in physical appearance and personality characteristics between Jack and Andy Griffith's fictional television character, Andy Taylor of Mayberry, but they realized the adventurous life of *Forrest Gump*, also a fictional character, had many similarities to their dad as well (in both the movie and the book). Jack was from a small town, in his late teens he served in the U.S military during the Vietnam War, Jack entered a career in which he rescued people but never boasted about it, he met a future U.S. president, he lived his life trying to do the right thing, he had a strange encounter with movie stars, he was a fishing boat captain, he sang in the choir, he experienced dating a woman who was pregnant by another man, he cut grass on a rider mower, and he used the term "Hot Damn" — much of which occurred many years before Winston Groom penned the book, *Forrest Gump*. Jack unexpectedly witnessed and/or participated in historic events and high-profile news stories, then he stored documentation of his adventures in a piece of vintage Samsonite luggage, like the fictional character, Forrest, later did with a briefcase. Vickie's new revelation did not change the way Andy Taylor of Mayberry reminded them of Jack, but from that point on, Forrest Gump would simply be another reminder of how amazing they believed their dad was.

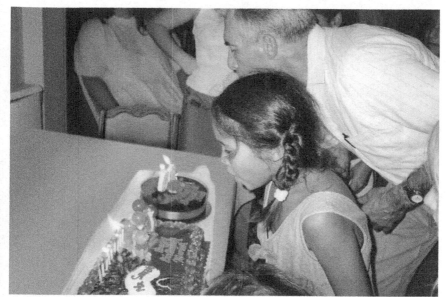

Jack sharing a birthday party with his granddaughter, Moriah, at Vickie's house in 1999

Jack with Vickie and his granddaughters, Moriah and Jordan, outside of Cornucopia diner, Oroville, Calif., 2010

Jack holding his first granddaughter, Courtney, 1988

Jack with his granddaughter, Courtney, on a Father's Day river boat cruise, Suisun City, Calif., 2010

*Jack holding his first great-granddaughter, Kalli, in a booth at the Cornu-
copia diner, 2011*

Little Jackie Smith Became…

CHAPTER THIRTEEN
One with God

On July 3, 2012, Vickie shared a post on her Facebook page from the *Today Show*. It was listed as breaking news with the following headline: "America's sheriff Andy Griffith has died at age 86." He reportedly died of a heart attack at his home in North Carolina. With the Facebook post, Vickie wrote, "I liked Andy Griffith. And, Sheriff Andy Taylor always reminded me of my dad. So sad."

Vickie's friend, Theresa, a Black woman who joked when she and Vickie were young that Jack was a white man she wanted to marry, responded to Vickie's post about Andy Griffith by writing, "You know he has ALWAYS reminded me of Jack and I have ALWAYS had a crush on both of them!!!" Vickie's friend, Stephanie, whose husband informed her of Andy Griffith's passing, also responded to Vickie's post. Stephanie wrote, "Jim JUST told me of his passing...I've been whistling the theme song for the Andy Griffith show since;)!!! You're SO RIGHT, HE DOES remind me of your Dad!!..."

Eleven days later, in Oroville, Jack loaded a basket of dirty clothes into his car for his weekly Saturday morning trip to a local laundromat. It was usually an uneventful experience, but this day was different. While Jack's clothes were in the dryer, a woman was walking through a parking lot on the west side of the laundromat when she noticed an elderly man sitting in a car. He appeared to be unconscious. The woman called 911, and three Oroville police officers responded to the scene. They found a man sitting in the front driver's seat of a car with the driver's side door propped open. According to the police report, "The man's legs were positioned outside."

The unresponsive man had no pulse and was not breathing, but he was warm to the touch, so two of the police officers removed the man from the car, placed him on the ground, and began CPR until paramedics arrived and took over. The paramedics continued CPR until they arrived at Oroville Hospital. With medical tubing placed in the man's mouth and arms, doctors continued to attempt to revive him, but to no avail. The man was declared dead at 10:59 A.M. He was identified by his California driver's license as a local man, seventy-two-year old Jack Smith of Oroville.

Though there were no visible signs of trauma, the cause of Jack's death was considered suspicious because his body was discovered in his car that was parked between a laundromat and a bank. The Butte County Sheriff's Department took possession of Jack's body and impounded his car and Jack's wallet, checkbook, cell phone, wristwatch, pocketknife, keys, and $29.55 in cash, which were booked as Coroner's Property. Jack, the former Butte County deputy sheriff, detective, and team leader for Search and Rescue had, himself, become a Butte County Sheriff's Department case number.

A Butte County sheriff's deputy searched through Jack's cell phone and called the first number in the contact list. The person who answered the phone identified herself as Jack's daughter, Vickie. In the coroner's report, the deputy wrote, "I notified Vicki of the decedent's death at that time." The officer then wrote, "Vicki was unable to speak after being notified of the decedent's death, and I spoke with her husband, Glen."

A short time later, Alan and his wife, Isela, arrived at Vickie's house. Vickie answered the door and fell into her brother's arms. Both were in shock and in tears. That night, still sobbing, Vickie cried herself to sleep. She awoke two hours later in tears again. Vickie left her bed and sat on the couch in her living room, the same seat in which her dad sat only a few weeks earlier when he was at her home to celebrate Father's Day. Occasionally, in the years prior, Jack had talked about moving out of Oroville because the population had doubled since he first arrived there in 1955. Vickie felt as though her dad made good on his plans to leave Oroville, but instead of a moving to small mountain-town, he went to heaven. Vickie sat on the couch and cried, talked to God, cried some more, talked to her dad, dozed off, then woke up in tears and repeated it all over again.

Vickie didn't know the cause of Jack's death, though she suspected it may have had something to do with prior heart trouble he had experienced — heart trouble that she thought, for the most part, had been resolved. And Vickie didn't want to think about her dad's last conscious moments — which no one seemed to have witnessed — but what did replay in her mind was the story she was told about the scene of the police and paramedics attempting to revive her dad. After Jack was seen sitting unconscious in his car outside the laundromat and 911 was called, fire trucks, law enforcement automobiles, and an ambulance all swarmed the area. To accommodate space needed for all the emergency vehicles, at least one lane of the main street, Oro Dam Boulevard, was blocked, and traffic was diverted. Jack's second wife, Patricia, was caught in the traffic that morning, and had seen the emergency vehicles, but, until later, did not know the incident involved Jack.

At first, Vickie felt bad because she knew her dad would not want to inconvenience the drivers on the road, and he certainly wouldn't want an audience for a scene like that, then Vickie panicked at the thought of the media having captured photos of the incident. In a small town like Oroville, it was quite possible for that type of situation to attract the news media—especially if they suspected it could have been the result of a crime, so, as daylight approached, Vickie sat on her couch with her computer turned on and between bouts of crying, nodding off, and waking in tears, she watched for online updates to the *Oroville Mercury* newspaper. Vickie worried that Jack's death might become the next news story he would be associated with, so she begged God not to let it be in the news. Vickie checked for updates throughout the day—and she found nothing. The following day, still nothing, and Vickie was relieved that there probably would be no story about her dad's public death in the news—not even a mention of his name. For a man who spent more than fifty years of his life repeatedly associated with news stories, Vickie felt the absence of such was nothing short of a miracle. Two days after Jack was founded deceased in his car, an investigation determined the cause of his death was not the result of foul play but rather heart failure.

When it came to arrangements for a funeral service, Jack didn't have written plans or a burial plot chosen, so Alan and Vickie had to figure it out on their own; they knew Jack would want to be laid to rest in Oroville, so they searched for a place they thought would be best. Traveling from one cemetery to the next, along with Vickie's husband, Glen, Alan and Vickie didn't see anything that felt right for their dad until the day they went to a location that overlooked Butte County. Standing on the hilltop cemetery, facing west, the coastal mountains could be seen in the distance straight ahead. Across the valley floor, the Sutter Butte Mountain Range was forty miles to the left; the iconic Table Mountain eleven miles to the right. The Oroville Dam, eight miles behind, could not be seen, but its presence could be felt. Old oak trees lined the rolling golden hills all around, and at the base of the hilltop where they stood were railroad tracks and a working lumber yard. Alan, Vickie, and Glen all stood in silence until Vickie said, "This is it." The others agreed.

More than a week after Jack's passing, and forty-five years after his name appeared with the announcement of the birth of his daughter as a statistic in the *Oroville Mercury* newspaper, an obituary was published and Jack's name and announcement of his death was listed under the statistics category well. The family included a photo of Jack taken several years earlier during a family gathering on a boat in the delta. In the photo, Jack was standing with his arm around one of his granddaughters—a time when he was at his happiest. The photo was cropped to create a headshot of Jack to display his beautiful smile. Upcoming funeral details were

Jack's obituary photo, 2012

given along with his name, Jack Lloyd Smith, and the follow-ing was written: "Overflowing with love, kindness, and gentle spirit, he is deeply loved and will be dearly missed."

The only words Jack ever said about what he wanted after he died were, "Just throw my ass in the fire and forget about it." So, Jack was cremated. Nine days later, his funeral was held graveside. The mid-morning in July was pleasant to the senses—comfortably warm with a slight breeze, the smell of fresh-cut lumber, and the occasional sound of a passing freight train. Guests were invited to sit in chairs under canopies or stand on the outskirts to say goodbye to Jack a final time while overlooking the community he loved and protected.

Jack's ashes were placed in an urn on a pedestal and put on display near the edge of one of the canopies. Flowers were placed several feet behind and to each side of the urn, and a podium was set up with a microphone for the pastor to lead the funeral. A folded American flag was placed on a stand behind the urn. To the right of the podium was a table with pictures of Jack and a shadow box displaying his service in the military and law enforcement. Members of the California Honor Guard stood nearby in preparation of playing Taps and presenting a triangular-folded American flag to Alan during the ceremony. Facing the urn, the podium, and the flowers, chairs were lined up beneath two canopies for guests to view the ceremony. The canopies and nearby trees shaded everything, but the urn and flowers shaped like a cross shone beautifully in the direct sunlight.

As the funeral start-time approached, guests filled the chairs, and some stood behind and to the sides of those who were seated. In addition to Jack's children, grandchildren, great-granddaughter, and his former stepdaughter, both of

Jack's ex-wives and their extended families were in attendance. Jack's longtime friends, Tony (and his wife), Roger and Dena, Jack's diner buddies, and others who had been friends with Jack for many years were there. Vickie's high school friends, Veronica and Angelique, were in attendance with their children, family members of Alan and Vickie's spouses were there, and so was Vickie's first husband, Dean, with his son from his second marriage. There also were many people from various law enforcement agencies, both former and current members of the Butte County Sheriff's Department, Oroville Police Department, the California Highway Patrol, California State Police, and the Butte County District Attorney's Office. Tim Taylor, the new Butte County School Superintendent, a man who only met Jack two months earlier, also came to pay his respects. Vickie's neighbor, Lily, would have attended Jack's funeral, but at age 101, she was still spunky, but not physically healthy enough for the long drive.

Several of the guests worked with Jack in some of his memorable or newsworthy events: Deputy Sumner watched Jack stand in a field without protective gear to talk a man into dropping a weapon with which he had only minutes before shot himself in front of his young daughter and fired two shots at paramedics; Sheriff's Department dispatcher Mary Jane Perrucci communicated with Jack by radio as he chased Butte County Jail escapees through the Feather River Canyon; Deputy Butch Ellis, who was in the passenger seat of Jack's speeding patrol car on a blood run. Also in attendance was the widow of Jack's former colleague, Deputy Hageman; she was the laboring woman who Jack surprised in 1969 by sitting in for her husband at the hospital and whose toe Jack squeezed through each contraction until she was transferred to a delivery room.

The guests, alone, could have been a testament to the type of person Jack was, but Jonathan Zachariou (the evangelical pastor and family friend who, with the Armenian priest, Father Hairabedian, married Vickie and her second husband, Glen, ten years earlier) knew Jack well and was asked to officiate the funeral because Vickie knew he would deliver the right words to describe her dad—and he did just that! The pastor began by declaring that Jack trusted his life to the Lord and was in the presence of his heavenly Father; it was the fruit of his faith. And, in fact, faith was a large part of Jack's life. Though some things may have temporarily shaken that faith over the years, most days, Jack knew deep down that everything was going to be okay. Even as a teenager, Jack knew his mother's signet ring, his Samsonite suitcase, and documents weren't the only things worth saving in life—his soul was too. Jack accepted God's invitation in high school, he was baptized, and there was no doubt to anyone who knew Jack and believed in heaven, that Jack had gone there for his final adventure.

Kindness shined from Jack's eyes, love from his smile, patience from his gentle touch, and the simple sound of his voice gave people a feeling of calm. Anxiety would ease when he arrived to break up a bar fight, injured people would sigh relief when he responded to the scene of an accident, and frightened victims of domestic violence would relax at the sound of his reassuring voice. Jack's gift of comfort may have been why God chose to place him on a U.S. Navy ship during the Laos Crisis, in the labor room with his friend's frightened wife, in Alaska at the time of the Exxon Valdez spill, and during the turbulent times in Belgrade and Moscow, with his children and grandchildren when they needed reassurance and guidance, and in countless other places over the span of his life. Pastor Jonathan described Jack by saying, "I don't know of a man who has better loved his neighbor."

Pastor Jonathan spoke of how Jack loved everyone he had contact with and said that wherever Jack went he was friends with people, the people just didn't know it yet. Pastor Jonathan also spoke of how Jack taught us how to treat each other, and how he didn't shy away from helping others. Pastor referred to the commandment to love your neighbor as you love yourself, and added, "There's not enough to be said about Jack, and there's really not enough to be said about a man's commitment to wanting to walk in good character."

When explaining the difference between personality, something we're born with, and character, something that is our choice, Pastor Jonathan knew Jack's one-year-old great-granddaughter, Kalli, loved to eat, so he used her as an example of personality. Pastor explained that, as a one-year-old, Kalli's love of food is like something people are born with, and as people mature, character is how we choose to dress that personality. Pastor Jonathan said, "He was an extraordinarily unique man, in that way; a man who should be emulated." With a slight pause in between each word, to emphasize his point, Pastor continued, Jack-fashioned-his-character-beautifully; he was an amazingly crafted, good-character man."

Just then, while Pastor so eloquently described Jack's faith and "amazingly crafted, good character," two hummingbirds appeared in flight from the area where the hill dropped down, about 20 feet behind Pastor Jonathan. The hummingbirds flew to a nearby tree, and a moment later, one of the hummingbirds left the tree, flew behind the pastor's head again, then straight toward the people at the service. The hummingbird flew over and passed the flower arrangements, then it stopped and hovered over Jack's urn — facing the guests.

Alan was sitting in the front row next to the center aisle with his wife, Isela, and Vickie's daughters and granddaughter to their far right. Vickie was sitting in the front row across the center aisle from Alan with her husband seated to her immediate left and her mom to her far left. Only a few feet away from the hummingbird, Vickie stared at it. She wasn't sure if anyone else was paying attention to the hummingbird until she heard gasps from the other guests.

The hummingbird remained hovered over Jack's urn and appeared to be staring at all the guests. About fifteen seconds later, the hummingbird turned back in the direction from which it came, flew behind the pastor's head to the tree where the other hummingbird appeared to be waiting, and the two hummingbirds flew off together. All the while, unaware of the hummingbirds, Pastor Jonathan continued speaking, and though a bit stunned by the behavior of the hummingbird, the attention of the guests was, once again, directed back him.

No one who knew Jack could dispute the words Pastor Jonathan used to describe him — if not from personal experience but because others, who had never met the pastor and were not present at the funeral, said the same thing in private conversations. After Jack's passing, Glen Toney, Jack's friend in high school, told Vickie during a phone conversation that even as a teenager, Jack was a nice, handsome young man with a warm smile and high-quality character, and he carried himself with dignity. Also, after Jack passed away, Richard Carl Napuuone DeMello, a man who worked in Alaska with Jack in the 1980s, told Vickie that when thinking of Jack, it was his character that came to mind.

Additionally, no one who knew Jack could argue that despite a tragic childhood, Jack set the bar high for himself in decency, in integrity, in unconditional love, in spirituality, and in self-control, and no matter the heartbreak, the disappointment, the setbacks, the challenges, or even the adventure he was on, Jack never lowered that bar. Jack would confess that he didn't always meet the standards he set for himself, but everyone admired the fact that Jack met them far more often than he fell short. Simply through living by example, Jack taught people a lot about life, and while he was making tough situations appear simple, he knew deep down how difficult it really was to do the right thing, so he didn't judge others' faults harshly.

Periodically, during the funeral service, Pastor lightheartedly referred to how much he enjoyed the pies Jack would bring to social gatherings at Vickie's house. Each time, it invoked a bit of laughter from the guests; it also set the stage for the time the service was nearing an end and Pastor Jonathan invited guests to use his microphone to share some words about their experiences with Jack. A family friend, Jennifer, was the first to speak. She talked about the Christmas cards Jack sent every year and how surprised she was that a single man of his age was so diligent about sending Christmas cards that always had something meaningful written inside — Jennifer called the cards, "…just an 'I love you.'" She mentioned the pies, and added, "I'm really going to miss his smile, his hugs…and his unconditional love." Jennifer reminded the guests that Jack's legacy lives on in his children and grandchildren. She said, "Just look in their eyes."

The next speaker was Tim Taylor, one of Vickie's former bosses and the new Butte County Superintendent of Schools, and who, at Vickie's urging, met with Jack for pie at Cornucopia when he first accepted his new job in Butte County. Tim Taylor was moving from Sacramento to Oroville, and Vickie knew her dad would be able to introduce Tim to the city and the people of Oroville. At Jack's funeral, Tim Taylor walked to the microphone with a Cornucopia pie in hand, and said, "I'm different than anyone here. I met Jack one time, about seven weeks ago…some people you meet in your life and you just go, 'Wow! That's a good guy!'" Tim Taylor told a few stories of his meeting with Jack, offered his best to Vickie and her family, and then walked to Vickie's seat, hugged her, and handed her the pie.

Vickie's sister-in-law, LeeAnn, spoke next. She talked about Jack becoming part of the family when Glen and Vickie got married, and that "…he embraced us so completely and so beautifully…" LeeAnn spoke about lots of memories spent with Jack at family gatherings, and lots of pies, thanks to

Jack."

The current Butte County sheriff, Jerry Smith, walked to the microphone next. He opened by saying, "Unfortunately, Jack didn't give me a pie." The guests laughed. He continued, "What he did give me, however, was some time to spend with him at our 'old-timers' function."

Vickie wondered if jokes about Jack's recent law-breaking incidents—like the ticket he was given for speeding, another ticket for driving without a seatbelt, and then a third ticket for driving while holding his cell phone to his ear (all of which Jack could have name-dropped people in law enforcement as an attempt to get out of trouble, but he didn't)—might surface at his funeral. But nothing was mentioned. Instead, the sheriff kept the remainder of his words short and serious. He looked at Jack's children seated in the first row of chairs, pointed toward the people standing at the back of the canopies, and said, "On behalf of the Butte County Sheriff's Office, myself, and others, a number of them are back there, we wanted to wish the family well, and you've always got a family with the sheriff."

Vickie's cousin, Brenda, spoke of times spent with Jack in the 1970s when she and Vickie were young, and how much she loved her Uncle Jack. Others also used Jack's passing as an opportunity to share memories about him. Jack's former stepdaughter, Lori, talked about how good Jack was to her—even after Jack and her mother divorced. Jack's former colleagues at Butte County Sheriff's Department, Perry Reniff and Lee Scofield, both commented on how Jack was so emotionally impacted by the cases he worked on, he couldn't leave them at work when his shift ended — his mind took the cases home with him. Lee Scofield's wife, Shirley, had a innocent crush on her husband's former colleague, Jack, and jokingly told Vickie's cousin, "If I wasn't married, I would have chased Jack to the ends of the earth."

Carolyn, Ann's sister (and Jack's former sister-in-law) said Jack was always a sweetheart. Kevin, Rick, and Sonny (Ann's brother's, and Jack's former brothers-in-law) talked about Jack's kindness and shared stories about Jack from their younger years. Vickie's stepson, Aaron, expressed how much he enjoyed the lottery scratchers Jack put in the birthday and Christmas cards. Aaron also told the story of how he and Jack considered soupin' up Jack's Honda. Vickie's other stepson, Adam, and his wife, Chanya, shared Aaron's sentiments about the lottery scratchers. Adam said, "Every Christmas we would always do the scratchers. It was a lot of fun. That's probably one of my fondest memories of Grandpa Jack."

Vickie's cousin, Angel, told Vickie how much she loved her "Uncle Jack." Alan's sister-in-law, Cristian, spoke about what a gentleman Jack was and how he used to stand up to greet them, and that he used to give her mom little gifts. Vickie's father-in-law, Albert, mother-in-law, Antica, and Glen's brother-in-law, Jon, all described Jack as being a good guy. Even Kennedy, the twelve-year old daughter of Vickie's high school friend, Veronica, shared stories of seeing Jack at Vickie's house on countless occasions and how friendly "Mr. Smith" was. Finally, Jeanine, a waitress at Cornucopia, shared how much Jack meant to the people who served him every day at the diner, and how much he will be missed. Getting choked up, Jeanine said to Jack, "I hope you're happy wherever you are, and I know where the sun is shining, so are you."

When the funeral guests finished speaking about Jack, recording artist, Julianna Zachariou, a family friend who grew up in church with Vickie's daughters, approached the microphone and played her acoustic guitar while singing *Amazing Grace*. A cemetery worker then parked a small tractor filled with dirt next to a small hole in the ground. Jack's urn was placed inside, and the cemetery workers, with shovels in hand, prepared to cover it with dirt. But first, Alan and Vickie split a bouquet of roses between them and each placed the flowers into the hole and directly on top of Jack's urn. Next, using both of his hands, Pastor Jonathan scooped dirt from the back of the small tractor and sprinkled it into the hole and over the top of Jack's urn. Pastor was immediately followed by one of Jack's longtime friends who walked to the front from the seating area and also scooped dirt with his hand and sprinkled over the top of Jack's urn. Next in line for a scoop of dirt was Vickie's husband, Glen, then Alan, and finally, Vickie; one-by-one, while drying tears from their eyes, each spread a handful of dirt over Jack's urn.

Cemetery workers filled the hole with the remaining dirt while Pastor Jonathan led the service in a final prayer. Immediately after the prayer, the funeral director read scripture and gave his closing remarks. Just then, before two of Jack's favorite songs, the Spinners' *Rubberband Man* and *Games People Play* officially ended the service, a man's voice broke the silence from the seating area behind the family. The unidentified man was heard saying, in a somber tone, "Goodbye, Jack."

Many of the guests left the funeral immediately after the service ended, but among those who remained, the appearance of the hummingbird was a topic of discussion. Everyone who saw the bird believed it represented a spiritual or heavenly moment involving Jack. Vickie believed it had something to do with her dad being near, and Alan did too. Even Vickie's colleague, Lisa, a person who had never met Jack but came to the funeral to support Vickie, said she saw the hummingbird, nudged the man she was standing next to, and said, "Jack!"

Pastor Jonathan explained to Vickie that God sometimes uses animals to remind us that our loved ones are with Him — which explained why so many people at the funeral felt a Godly presence during the hummingbird visit. However, Vickie was still confused as to how, in addition to feeling God's presence with the hummingbird, she also felt her dad's presence. Later, Vickie surmised that because Jack was one with God on earth, that oneness remained when he died, so his presence was represented in the hummingbird as well.

Sunset view from Jack's hilltop gravesite, 2012

EPILOGUE

I started writing this book in the early 2000s, an idea inspired by those who expressed an interest in what became of Little Jackie Smith after his mother's suicide. At the time, I knew there were a lot of interesting things about my dad's life after his mother's tragic death, and I suspected there was a lot more I didn't know. I was right, and twenty years after publishing my grandmother's biography, I finally put my dad's life story into book form as well.

If my dad had lived to see his biography completed, he would know and would understand why it took me so long to finish. Before he passed, my dad graciously accommodated my requests for information, as I shifted the ideas of the book from non-fiction to fiction and back again, at least once. I finally decided there was no need to write fiction — my dad's reality was interesting enough — but then came my dilemma of how to format the chapters of his life story.

I researched and wrote mostly on holidays or summer breaks. Sometimes I got so excited with an idea, I wrote throughout an entire holiday period and then in my spare time after work over the span of several months, only to dislike the way the story flowed, scrap what I had done, take a break, then start all over again in a new direction. This occurred numerous times over a period of several years, and through it all, my dad left it entirely up to me. He never made suggestions about the way his life story should be written. Instead, he patiently followed me down one path and then another and another. My dad always complimented my ideas, supported my work in any way he could, and never questioned what I thought was best.

Part of the delay in completion of my dad's book was also due to obligations I had to normal life, and sometimes to not-so-normal, rare and unlikely events that occasionally occurred in my life—many of which my dad could see similarities to his own. For example, on numerous occasions, I was put in situations in which I had to fight to expose wrongdoing—some requiring years of battle. I also occasionally struggled in my faith and contemplated doing the right thing, and, like my dad, when I gave in to both, it all worked out. When I didn't give in to both, things got worse, and I tried harder the next time.

Thankfully, not all of the rare and unlikely events I experienced were difficult. Some, like many of my dad's, were thrilling. In addition to the time my girls and I happened upon the Security Bank Building and ended up on the outside ledge—the same place from which my grandmother leapt to her death, later, I, too, like my dad, had a chance encounter with a television celebrity who entered politics and held an administrative position in the White House—not as president, but the president's daughter and one of his closest advisors, Ivanka Trump.

Also, like when my dad worked as a tour guide for members of the U.S. Senate during his time in Alaska, I, too, was involved in an event with congressmen. The more interesting parts of my story, however, occurred several years later when one of those congressmen, Anthony Weiner, a member of the U.S. House of Representatives (who was sitting directly behind me at the event), ended his career in a high-profile sexting scandal—one that landed him in prison. Another congressman at the event, Chuck Schumer, had been a member of the U.S. House of Representatives before being elected as a U.S. Senator. Several years later, as a high-profile member of his party, he became the Senate Majority Leader. And lastly, like my dad, I, too, was associated with or appeared in local media, mostly television. Sometimes it was planned, but other times it happened by surprise.

Adding to my normal, and not-so-normal, life, and the inability to decide on a format for the chapters, another contributor to the delay in completing my dad's biography was the crushing blow I felt from losing him—a parent I relied on for guidance, protection, and unconditional love. After my dad's passing, I feared having to navigate my way through life without him, so I dealt with it by trying to keep him alive in any way I could. Some would say my delay in completing the book was one of the ways I chose to keep him alive, and if that was the case, it wasn't intentional—though there was some comfort in going back in time through writing and researching his life story. What I did do intentionally was dedicate my time to ways I felt were important to keeping my dad's memory alive. For example, just months after my dad passed away, I mailed Christmas cards for him (those he had already prepared before his death, about half of those on his annual list), I began giving Cornucopia pies to family and friends on holidays, and with the help of my colleagues at the school for at-risk youth—Bradford, Marla, Renee, Adrian,

Kevin, Sandra, Ty, SCOE school district (my employer), and members of the Sacramento County Probation Department— I started an annual Thanksgiving Pie Giveaway for needy families.

The summer following my dad's passing, I also started a memorial scholarship fund in my dad's name at the Butte College Police Academy. The scholarship provides a small amount of money to one cadet in each graduating class who has, throughout the time in the academy, demonstrated exceptional character. And I have kept my dad's memory alive by continuing, despite the obstacles, to write his biography.

My daughters also chose to honor their Grandpa Jack's memory in ways they felt important. Courtney, my oldest daughter, gave birth to her first child ten months after my dad's passing. She named her newborn son, Jack, in honor of the grandfather she adored. Moriah, my middle daughter, had an exact replica of her Grandpa Jack's closing line on letters and cards, "All My Love," tattooed on her shoulder blade. Jordan, my youngest daughter, who started riding horses at the age of eight, and who owned her own horse at the time of my dad's passing, continued to ride and care for horses after he passed away—a passion she shared with her Grandpa Jack.

If my dad was still living, he could have continued helping me throughout the completion of his biography, and if he was still living, I probably wouldn't have as many lingering unanswered questions as I do. For example, having ordered some of my dad's military records after he passed away, I

Courtney with Baby Jack

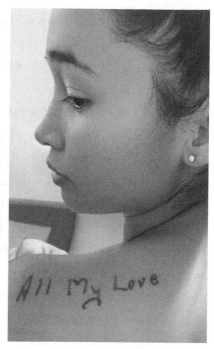

Moriah's tattoo of Jack's handwriting

Jordan with her horse (photo courtesy of Steve Pate-Newberry)

discovered his admittance to having suffered from a stutter as a child. My dad always gave me the impression that he made it through his childhood without any signs of trauma – this was potential evidence to the contrary. Also, after my dad's passing, I dug further into the items stored in his Samsonite, and I found a newspaper clipping from the *Anchorage Daily News* dated October 1986. The headline story was titled, "A Spectacular – and safe – landing: Pilot brings 727 from Prudhoe Bay down without benefit of landing gear." An accompanying photo showed a plane sitting on tarmac with the nose gear touching the ground. I don't remember my dad ever telling a story about being on a plane during an emergency landing, but I knew it must have been the airplane that carried him back and forth between Prudhoe Bay and Anchorage every two weeks or so when he worked in Alaska.

In hopes of finding a passenger list, I contacted the NTSB and the FAA, but nothing could be located. If my dad was on the flight, it would have fallen right in line with some of the other craziness he experienced, like unknowingly walking into the middle of convenience store robbery, strolling down a street in Italy when a car bomb exploded, or stumbling upon a family secret, to name a few. Whatever happened with the emergency landing of the airplane, dad felt the news article was important enough to hold onto. There were 109 passengers onboard, and as one of the passengers reported to the newspaper, "…everybody knows everyone," so even if my dad wasn't on the plane for that flight in particular, I'm certain he knew some of the people who were, but I may never know for certain one way or the other.

There was one thing I found in my dad's possessions that didn't need explaining. He enjoyed stories of people who displayed strength when it wasn't always expected of them, those who were, far too often, perceived of as weak or less-than-capable (like women, minorities, or social outcasts like the ones in San Francisco who cared for him when he was twelve-years old). After my dad passed away, I found a small newspaper clipping about a woman in Russia who walked too closely to a bear and her cubs. The bear attacked the woman, and while it had one of the woman's hands gripped in its' teeth, the Russian woman, a retired postal worker, used her good hand to beat the bear until it released her injured hand. I could easily imagine my dad laughing when he read the story, tearing the clipping out of the newspaper, folding it, and placing it inside his wallet—which is where it remained until he died.

With the downsides of not having my dad around, I do recognize, in his absence, there are some things I included in my dad's life story after he passed away that added a different perspective because I obtained the information from sources I likely would not have otherwise sought. For example, if my dad was still living, I would have continued to only turn to him for information, because I truly believed he was able to give me all of the information I needed to know, and I wouldn't have felt a need to interview anyone else. But, without my dad, I was forced to seek information in new ways from new people, and as a result, I discovered things about my dad he may not have remembered, may not have thought to tell me, may not have known, or did not want to tell me out of respect for another person.

In addition to researching historical documents, I sought interviews with people who knew my dad well. Through these discussions, my dad's exceptional character was confirmed, both for me and the person I was interviewing. For example, when I interviewed dad's long-time friend, Tony, we got into a discussion about how my parents met, which was prior to when he first met my dad. I told Tony the story of my parents' chance meeting at the Thrifty Diner and how awesome my dad was for still wanting to date my mom even though she was in the first trimester of her pregnancy with Alan. Tony informed me that he never knew Alan wasn't Jack's biological child, and as though he knew it fit my dad's character like a glove, Tony said, "For Jack, some things were worth talking about."

Also, through my research, I gained personal insight into what Oroville was like when my dad was in high school, and what some of my dad's high school friends thought of him. I was told stories by people who had been my dad's law enforcement colleagues in the 1970s, the 1980s, and the 1990s, and by people who shared decades-long friendships with him. As a result, I learned details to incidents I knew little about and to things I had never known. I was also given first-hand accounts of what life was like in Fort Bragg when my dad was a fisherman on his boat, the *Ramona R.* My mom opened up to me about their marriage, which she had never really done, and knowing I was aware that she didn't like my dad for the first few years after their divorce, she wanted me to know that overall, she thought my dad was a good man.

My dad's second wife, Patricia, shared stories with me as well, and she confirmed the way I, too, felt about him when she said, "Having him around was like having a security blanket."

After my dad passed away, ideas about how to write his biography continued to bounce around in my head. I used my dad's laptop in hopes it would give me inspiration, and though using it to write was meaningful to me, it didn't help with much progress for the book. Making things even more difficult, I was in mourning, which was obvious in some of my writing, so a lot of what I wrote in the first couple of years after my dad's passing had to be deleted and or rewritten. That's also the time when I came to the realization that I included too much about myself in my dad's life story, and added too many personal opinions, so I kicked myself out of writing in first person and decided to write in third person instead.

Late in the year of 2016, four years after my dad passed away, I chose a format for the layout of the book, and I stuck to it. The final idea was inspired by a song titled *Something Worth Saving* by Gavin DeGraw, a track from an album of the same title that he released in 2016. *Something Worth Saving* was likely written with romance in mind, but I saw it differently. Instead of romantic love, many of the lyrics of the song reminded me of my dad and me. The verses of the song tell the story of two people who accomplished a lot together, and when things got a little crazy and then calmed back down, those two people were still standing together. That's how I felt after my dad went to heaven; he and I had worked together on his mom's biography and on his life story, and we accomplished more than either of us dreamed of, but when my dad passed away, I felt like a big part of my life had exploded. Then, in the years to follow, as the dust settled, I was still working on our project and I felt as if my dad was still standing right by my side.

The title and the lyrics of the chorus in *Something Worth Saving* also reflected other aspects of my life and of my dad's life. The song tells a story in which some things are worth saving, even if it breaks the heart to do so. There were many times when I was writing my dad's life story after his passing that I became so distraught at having lost him, I had to take a break from writing. I always returned, however, because deep down, I knew that his life story was worth documenting and saving, and that finishing it would be worth any pain it caused me. I also realized that the song described my dad as well; he saved memorabilia even if they were heartbreaking events or brought back painful memories, like the sinking of the *Ramona R.* or the news coverage of his mother's suicide, because in his mind, they were things worth saving along with the happy and exciting memories. I remember listening to the chorus of *Something Worth Saving* and thinking, "That's us! That's what we do! 'We save things!'" That's when I decided to format the chapters of my dad's life story based on the items he stored in his Samsonite.

I initially presumed my dad's life story would be mostly independent of his mother's story. Afterall, most of what I was writing about occurred after she died. But, along the way, I realized my grandmother was very much a part of my dad's entire life. If not through the photos my dad kept of her, the signet ring with his initials engraved on it, or my name, then through the constant remake of the song "Blue Moon." In the end, rather than being independent of *Victoria's Secret: A Conspiracy of Silence*, my dad's life story turned out to be an extension of his mother's biography. The continuation of a true story.

Also, in writing my dad's life story, I expected to recap some of his younger years, but mostly tell the story of the man known as Jack. After all, shortly after his mother died, he no longer wanted to be called Little Jackie, or even Jackie; as a preteen, he chose to leave that name in his childhood. But, the more I researched and wrote, I realized that Little Jackie was not entirely left in childhood. I found that in my dad's adult life, there was still a little boy, Jackie, inside of him. I noticed it in the softening tone of my dad's voice in the mid-1990s when he first shared stories of his childhood with me for my college class assignment. It was even more obvious the day I first saw my dad after my grandmother's book was published, and I mailed a copy to him. He was standing outside the doors to the diner, Cornucopia, waiting for my daughters and me to arrive for a planned lunch date, and as my daughters and I walked toward him from our car, he looked at us with a smile on his face unlike any I had ever seen; I could swear I saw a thrilled little boy standing there instead of the man I had always known as my dad. It choked me up.

A few years later, I got a glimpse of Little Jackie again. It was during one of the times in the early 2000s when I was considering writing my dad's book as fiction, and I asked my dad to write a story about what type of scenario he envisioned if his mother had not jumped from the building — but, rather, if she had gotten the support she needed, continued to look for him, and if she would have located and retained custody of him, even if it took a few years. I wanted to know what my dad thought would happen when they saw each other again. The story my dad wrote as an adult appeared to be one from a child's perspective, and what became obvious was that throughout his life, a part of him remained Little Jackie, a loving son. On pages of lined paper, my dad handwrote:

> After dinner we decided to go for an early evening stroll. The weather was mild with clear skies. Walking down the sidewalk, chatting, holding hands, arms swinging, we came to a street crossing with a light pole and I suddenly remembered a game we used to play. "Hey Mom! Remember this?" I went on one side of the pole, she went on the other. Our hands parted then passed the pole and rejoined. In unison we hollered "Bread and butter go together" and we laughed. Further on, one could hear "bread and butter, bread and butter" followed with giggles or laughter.

> A city park was nearby so we crossed a couple more streets, saw a deli vendor at the entrance, got a couple of sodas and continued our evening stroll into the park as others were

doing. All the while talking about times gone by before and after the separation. Spotting an empty bench just off the pathway, we decided to sit for a while and enjoy the peaceful surroundings, watch the lights in the shops being turned down as darkness enveloped all around us. Sitting there sipping on our sodas in moment of silent reflections, she, with the gentle nature of a mother to soothe and caress her young, began lightly stroking the nape of my neck and back of my head. While Mom continued her gentle caresses, she began humming the melody to an old familiar song. Her favorite of those bygone years. "Blue Moon, you saw me standing alone, without a dream in my heart, without a love of my own." "Ah," she said, "oh yes," "there suddenly appeared before me, the only one my arms will ever hold. I heard somebody whisper please adore me and when I looked…"

Mom stopped humming, squeezed my neck while pointing with her soda cup. In front of us on the pathway were the shadows of us sitting on the bench. Mom then held up two fingers behind my head wiggling them like rabbit ears on my head. We chuckled and Mom said, "that made a cute silhouette." Then in a whispered, questioning tone, "She repeated the word, silhouette?" She turned to look over our shoulders, there was soft sigh. I looked at her and she had the sweetest most radiant teary-eyed expression I had ever seen. Following her gaze, I saw it and said, "Oh my!" Like the words of Mom's song—just above the horizon so full and bright was "the moon," shining like it "had turned to gold."

Since my dad's passing, I can't help but wonder if a scenario like the one my dad so eloquently wrote may have played out in a similar fashion when he got to heaven. There was a second hummingbird at my dad's funeral; maybe that one represented my grandmother. If God uses animals to remind us our loved ones are with Him, who's to say He doesn't use animals to remind us that our loved ones are also with each other?

Speaking of hummingbirds, they were a lot more meaningful to me after my dad's funeral, especially when I saw them on special occasions, like in my front yard on my birthday, or hovering outside the hospital room window when Courtney was in labor with Baby Jack. I also saw hummingbirds at random and uneventful times—a pattern that was similar, I suppose, to when I would have seen my dad if he was still here on earth—just less frequent.

Because of what happened with the hummingbird at my dad's funeral, my family and I (and some of our friends) subsequently believed the appearance of a hummingbird, any hummingbird, meant my dad was with God, and his presence was near us. For me, personally, the symbolism of the hummingbird became even more apparent a year after my dad's funeral. I was driving near my home, out running errands, while listening to a '70s music station on the radio, as I often did. When the Carpenters' song *(They Long to Be) Close to You* began playing on the radio, the childhood image of my dad came to mind, then, I also thought of his funeral, and it struck me! Birds actually did suddenly appear, just like the lyrics of the song! I was excited, because only God and I knew about the about the association I made as a child between that song and my dad, and of all the animals God could have used that day to remind us that my dad was with Him and near to us, God chose birds. That was it! I needed no more convincing about the significance of the humming-bird—and that, combined with the song, as far as I was concerned, God gave me a little extra comfort for my deep state of mourning.

During my dad's funeral, Rebekah, a family friend who was the videographer for the day, just happened to pause the camera (as she did periodically through the service) at the time of the hummingbird's visit, though she did capture a brief moment of the two hummingbirds together in flight. After my dad's funeral, regardless of how or when I saw hummingbirds, they remained elusive to a camera; either the hummingbird appeared when I didn't have my cell phone accessible, or it would fly off so quickly, I wasn't able to get a good picture.

That changed on July 14, 2019. It was the seven-year anniversary date of my dad's passing. That morning, I got into my car with a bouquet of roses, and, as I had done several times each year, I headed to my dad's grave. Accompanying me that day was my oldest daughter, Courtney, my nearly eight-year old grand-daughter, Kalli, my six-year old grandson, Jack, and my three-year-old grandson, Isaac.

The seventy-five-mile drive from Sacramento to Oroville went as planned until about half-way through our trip when my tire started going flat on the highway. Thankfully, I was near the town of Marysville, so I was able to drive to a tire shop and get the flat repaired. The delay took two hours out of our trip, and I thought about turning around and just taking the kids back home, but ultimately, I refused to let the incident deter me from honoring my dad on that day of remembrance.

Courtney, the three kids, and I arrived at my dad's hilltop gravesite later than expected, but, thankfully, before the sun went down. Much like the day of my dad's funeral, the

Vickie with three of her grandchildren, Kalli, Jack, and Isaac, at Jack's grave, 2019

weather was sunny, and comfortably warm. We put flowers on my dad's headstone, took pictures, and hung out for a short time; Courtney took a picture of the kids and me from my dad's grave, then we watched the kids roam around while we admired the scenery. In the years following my dad's funeral, I had always hoped to see a hummingbird appear at his grave again, but in all the times I visited, it never happened.

When it was time to leave, Courtney and I strapped the kids into their car seats in the back, and we situated ourselves in the front. I was in the driver's seat, so I placed my cell phone on the dashboard holder, and just as I began to drive away, I heard my cell phone buzz. I looked down and saw a notification on the screen from the security camera at my home — I ignored it. Moments later, my phone buzzed again. This time, it was a text from my husband urging me to look at the security camera footage. Curious, I came to a stop, still in the cemetery, and logged in to see what set off the motion sensor on one of our outdoor home security cameras. What I saw was something so unexpected my dad would have referred to it, like many incidents in his own life, as "unique in its own right," and because of the timing, he would have stated it happened "as if on cue."

What occurred seventy-five miles away, at the moment we were leaving my dad's grave on the seventh anniversary of his passing, a hummingbird flew within inches of my outdoor security camera, triggered the motion sensor, hovered for a moment, flew toward the front of my home, and then to a nearby tree before disappearing out of sight.

Hummingbird caught on security camera at Vickie's house, 2019

I was so excited, I responded to my husband's text with "OMG, that's so cool!" followed by two of the most important words my dad ever taught me, "Save it!"

ACKNOWLEDGEMENTS

Writing this book was a labor of love. I thank God for inspiration, guidance, strength, ambition, mercy, and grace — I could not have done this without Him. I thank my immediate and extended family for their unending support, and for loving my dad enough to accept my decades-long obsession with completing his life story. I thank my work family for understanding why I declined so many offers to work extra hours. I thank Jay and my church family for lots of prayers and laughter, and for lifting my spirits when I was in mourning and had a difficult time writing. I thank Kim and all my local friends for giving me confidence, and for understanding when my writing-time interfered with our girl-time. I thank Ellen, Natasha, Chandra, and all my friends afar for loving me over the years despite the distance and the limited contact due my writing.

Thanks to all my proofreaders, my husband, Glen (reader of many, many drafts), Kimberly Johnson, Chris Zachariou, Ashley Presnell, Perry Reniff, and Ann C. Leber.

Thanks to my editor and self-publishing coach/advisor, Rob Bignell, inventingrealityediting.com/home for assisting me through this process.

Thanks to Jim Courtis and my dad's other buddies at Cornucopia (and to the friends/acquaintances at the countless other diners my dad frequented over the span of his life). Thanks to Christina and all the staff at Cornucopia (and to the staff who served my dad at every other diner he like his frequented over the span of his life) for making my dad feel diner was a home-away-from-home. Thanks to all my dad's friends and colleagues, who, in his lifetime, supported and protected him.

I thank those who shared information with me, some are named in this book, others are not (for privacy reasons), and a special thanks to the memory of the following people who, through contact with me, contributed content to the stories told in this book, but did not live to see its' completion:

Almeda Avedikian

Thomas "Tommy" Ancona

Steven Kirk Bordwine, Jr.

Pearl Bohanon

Lydia Carvil

Richard Carl Napu'uone DeMello

Martin W. "Butch" Ellis

Mayo Goliti and other members of Goliti family

Fr. Yeghia Hairabedian

Lilian "Lily" Hutzler

Robert Markus

Lucy Saragosa

Raymond Lee Scofield

Elmer "Sonny" Smith

Retired Butte County Sheriff Jerry Smith

Renee Smith-Chiapa

Dr. Glen O. Toney

Grace Turner and other members of the Lazar family

...and last, but not least, Jack L. Smith

SELECTED BIBLIOGRAPHY

Chapter 1

"Blue Moon (1934 Song)." *Wikipedia*, Wikimedia Foundation, 11 Apr. 2021, en.wikipedia.org/wiki/Blue_Moon_(1934_song).

"Fresno, California." *Wikipedia*, Wikimedia Foundation, 2 Apr. 2021, en.wikipedia.org/wiki/Fresno,_California.

Jessup, Bryce, and Pat Gelsinger. *City on a Hill: William Jessup University Celebrates 75 Years of History*. Bryce Jessup, 2014.

Library, MTC-ABAG. *San Francisco County – 1950-1960 Census Data*, www.bayareacensus.ca.gov/counties/SanFranciscoCounty50.htm.

Oroville Mercury Register, 7 June 1957.

"Oroville, California." *Wikipedia*, Wikimedia Foundation, 14 Mar. 2021, en.wikipedia.org/wiki/Oroville,_California.

"Sacramento, California Population History 1860 - 2019." *Sacramento, California Population History | 1860 - 2019*, 12 Feb. 2021, www.biggestuscities.com/city/sacramento-california.

Sfcentric. "Once Upon A Time In The TL: Jazz At The Black Hawk Bar." *Hoodline*, 23 Oct. 2020, hoodline.com/2015/03/once-upon-a-time-in-the-tl-jazz-at-black-hawk-bar/.

"The Nuggett '57." Oroville Union High School Yearbook, 1957

"Weary, But Happy, The '57 Seniors Look Back As Commencement Day Nears." *Oroville Mercury Register*, 7 June 1957.

Chapter 2

"Carrier Crew Has Ample Facilities for Worship." *Long Beach Independent Newspaper*, 13 May 1961, p. 8.

"Day Late: Delay Arrival of Kearsarge." *Long Beach Independent Newspaper*, 17 Sept. 1961.

"Foreign and U.S. Ships Crisscross Ocean Lanes." *Long Beach Independent Newspaper*, 31 July 1961.

"Four Dead in 'Copter Crash." *Uniontown Evening Standard News*, 19 Sept. 1961, p. 9.

"Four Killed in Crash of Navy Helicopter." *Redlands Daily News*, 18 Sept. 1961, p. 1.

"John Turner Serves on Carrier, Kearsarge." *Auburn Journal Newspaper*, 22 June 1961, p. 19.

"Joyous Family Reunions Mark Kearsarge Return." *Long Beach Independent Newspaper*, 19 Sept. 1961, p. 6.

"Kearsarge III (CV-33)." *Naval History and Heritage Command*, 18 July 2020, www.history.navy.mil/research/histories/ship-histories/danfs/k/kearsarge-iii.html.

"The Laos Crisis, 1960–1963." *Office of the Historian*, U.S. Department of State, history.state.gov/milestones/1961-1968/laos-crisis.

Long Beach Independent Newspaper, 9 July 1961, p. 11.

"Navy Plane Crashes." *Kingsport News*, 11 May 1961, p. 6.

"Navy Task Force Heads for Orient." *Fairbanks Daily*

News-Miner, 27 Mar. 1961.

"Own Chapel Is Pride of Kearsarge Skipper." *Long Beach Independent Newspaper*, 23 Jan. 1961, p. 10.

"Rain or Caution Damps Laos War." *Santa Rosa Press Democrat*, 29 Mar. 1961, p. 4.

"Statistics." *Oroville Mercury Register*, 25 May 1967, p. 2.

"The Supremes Sing Rodgers & Hart (1967)." *THE DIANA ROSS PROJECT*, 2 Jan. 2016, dianarossproject.wordpress.com/2016/01/02/the-supremes-sing-rodgers-hart-1967/.

"The Supremes Sing Rodgers & Hart." *Wikipedia*, Wikimedia Foundation, 16 Feb. 2021, en.wikipedia.org/wiki/The_Supremes_Sing_Rodgers_%26_Hart.

"U.S. Military Forces On Move Across Pacific." *Harlington Valley Morning Star*, 30 Mar. 1961, p. 7.

"USS Kearsarge (CV-33)." *Wikipedia*, Wikimedia Foundation, 6 Apr. 2021, en.wikipedia.org/wiki/USS_Kearsarge_(CV-33).

"VS-21 'Fighting Redtails' Squadron History." *AMARC Experience*, www.amarcexperience.com/ui/index.php?option=com_content&view=article&id=134&catid=8&Itemid=159.

"With Anti-Sub Group." *The Chillicothe Constitution Tribune*, 20 June 1961, p. 11.

Chapter 3

Active NorCalNorthern California's Outdoor Digital Newsmagazine. "Remembering the Deadly Flood of 1955

That Put a NorCal Town Under 20 Feet of Water - Active NorCal." *Active NorCal - Telling the Stories of Northern California*, 6 Mar. 2019, activenorcal.com/remembering-the-deadly-flood-of-1955-that-put-a-norcal-town-under-20-feet-of-water/.

California, State of. "History." *Department of Water Resources*, 2021, water.ca.gov/Programs/State-Water-Project/SWP-Facilities/History.

"Flying into Oatman AZ!" *160knots.Com*, 16 July 2012, 160knots.com/Oatman.htm.

"The Lawless Have Laws." *Death Valley Days*, 1 Oct. 1965.

Lenhoff, James. *Oroville, California*. Arcadia Publishing, 2001.

Matthews, Larry R. *The Building of the Oroville Dam*. Arcadia Publishing, 2014.

Mifflin, Margot. *The Blue Tattoo: The Life of Olive Oatman*. University of Nebraska Press, 2011.

"Oatman, Arizona." *Wikipedia*, Wikimedia Foundation, 19 Mar. 2021, en.wikipedia.org/wiki/Oatman,_Arizona.

"Oroville Dam Had Problems from the Start in 1960's." *Sacramento Bee*, 14 May 2017.

"Oroville Dam." *Wikipedia*, Wikimedia Foundation, 22 Mar. 2021, en.wikipedia.org/wiki/Oroville_Dam.

"Oroville Is Sprucing Up For Big Dam Celebration." *Feather River Bulletin*, 18 Apr. 1968, p. 4.

Oroville Mercury Register, 1-6 May 1968.

"Table Mountain (Butte County, California)." *Wikipedia*, Wikimedia Foundation, 29 Sept. 2019, en.wikipedia.org/wiki/Table_Mountain_%28Butte_County_California%29.

Chapter 4

"Gridley Man Booked for Gould Murder." *Oroville Mercury Register*, 13 Sept. 1973, p. 1.

"Gridley Man Pleads Guilty to Second Degree Murder." *Oroville Mercury Register*, 2 Oct. 1973.

"Gridley Man Sentenced to Prison for Murder." *Oroville Mercury Register*, 19 Oct. 1973, p. 1.

"Innocent Plea Entered In Murder Case." *Oroville Mercury Register*, 17 Sept. 1973, p. 1.

"Riddle of the Hogtied Nude in the Creek." *Master Detective Magazine*, 1975, p. 40.

"Suicide Try Reported By Accused Slayer." *Oroville Mercury Register*, 1 Oct. 1973, p. 1.

"Woman's Bound Body Found Near Oroville." *Oroville Mercury Register*, 1 Sept. 1973, p. 1.

Chapter 5

"Andy Taylor (The Andy Griffith Show)." *Wikipedia*, Wikimedia Foundation, 12 Apr. 2021, en.wikipedia.org/wiki/Andy_Taylor_%28The_Andy_Griffith_Show%29.

"Biggs Youth Being Returned." *Oroville Mercury Register*, 18 July 1974, p. 1.

"Card Will Be Arraigned Monday." *Oroville Mercury Register*, 6 July 1974, p. 1.

"Coroner: Mrs. Judnick Died of Heart Attack." *Feather River Bulletin*, 25 Nov. 1974, p. 14.

"Deputy Chases YC Robbers, mid-late 1970's". Unknown Publication, unknown date.

"Dr. Gray's Assailant Gets Life Sentence." *Feather River Bulletin*, 28 Nov. 1974, p. 9.

"Extradition Paper Work Underway." *Oroville Mercury Register*, 16 July 1974, p. 14.

"George Gillick; Was Butte County Sheriff Who Never Had Gun." *Los Angeles Times*, Los Angeles Times, 22 Oct. 1988, www.latimes.com/archives/la-xpm-1988-10-22-mn-9-story.html.

"Gridley Youth Jailed in Judnick Shooting." *Oroville Mercury Register*, 12 July 1974, p. 1.

"Local Woman Shot; Two Suspects Sought." *Oroville Mercury Register*, 9 July 1974, p. 1.

"Mandatory Death Penalty Possible in Triple Slaying." *Oroville Mercury Register*, 8 July 1974, p. 1.

"Rock Throwing Sheriff Retires." *UPI*, UPI, 30 Dec. 1982, www.upi.com/achives/1982/12/30/rock-throwing-sheriff-retires/1235410072400/.

"Second Youth Jailed in Judnick Shooting." *Oroville Mercury Register*, 15 July 1974, p. 1.

"Shooting Victim's Condition Stable Following Brain Surgery Yesterday." *Oroville Mercury Register*, 10 July 1974, p. 1.

"Woman's Death Complicates Dr. Gray Assailants' Case." *Feather River Bulletin*, 21 Nov. 1974, p. 14.

"Woodcutter Arraigned in Slayings." *The Bakersfield Californian*, 10 July 1974, p. 54.

Chapter 6
"Bay Area Team Retrieves Body." *Oroville Mercury Register*,

29 Mar. 1976, p. 1.

"Beale Man Plunges Over Falls Lookout." *Oroville Mercury Register*, 26 Mar. 1976, p. 1.

"Feather Falls Area Searched for 2 Men." *Oroville Mercury Register*, 6 Feb. 1976, p. 1.

"One of Two Missing Found Dead in Hills." *Oroville Mercury Register*, 7 Feb. 1976, p. 1.

"Rescue Cost Said Not That Much." *Oroville Mercury Register*, 14 Feb. 1976, p. 1.

"Rescued Man Moved to Stanford Med Center." *Oroville Mercury Register*, 10 Feb. 1976, p. 1.

"Second Try Made to Recover Airman." *Oroville Mercury Register*, 27 Mar. 1976, p. 1.

"Willpower, Dog Keep Adams Alive 4 Days." *Oroville Mercury Register*, 9 Feb. 1976, p. 1.

Chapter 7

"Ex-Deputy Arraigned." *Oroville Mercury Register*, 6 Mar. 1976, p. 1.

"Feather Falls Area Searched For Plane." *Oroville Mercury Register*, 5 Apr. 1976, p. 1.

"Nine, Including Four Juveniles, Picked up on Burglary Charges." *Gridley Herald*, 24 Sept. 1975, p. 1.

"Pilot Disorientation Blamed For Crash." *Oroville Mercury Register*, Apr. 1976.

"Pilot's Body Recovered From Fall River Canyon." *Oroville Mercury Register*, Apr. 1976.

"Plane, Dead Pilot Found near Feather Falls." *Feather River Bulletin*, 8 Apr. 1976, p. 10.

Chapter 8

Department of Transportation. "Log Remarks Sheet." U.S. Coast Guard, Point Ledge, 21 May 1979.

"Noyo Problems." *The Ft. Bragg Advocate News*, 23 May 1979, p. 1.

"Noyo Problems." *The Mendocino Beacon*, 24 May 1979, p. 1.

Chapter 9

"The Alaska Spill: What Exxon Left Behind." *Newsweek Magazine*, 18 Sept. 1989, p. 50.

"ARCO Studies Claims Ex Workers Allege Slope Violations." *Anchorage Daily News*, 10 June 1988, p. B6.

"Cope on the Slope." *Anchorage Daily News*, 16 Aug. 1987, p. B1.

"Cowper, Hodel Chat about ANWR." *Fairbanks Daily News Miner*, 13 Aug. 1987.

Daylight and Darkness. 16 Oct. 2008, www.Alaska.com/2008/10/16/1920/daylight-and-darkness.html.

"Deadhorse Airport." Wikipedia, Wikimedia Foundation, 26 Mar. 2021, en.wikipedia.org/wiki/Deadhorse_Airport.

"Deadhorse, Alaska." *Wikipedia*, Wikimedia Foundation, 12 Feb. 2021, en.wikipedia.org/wiki/Deadhorse,_Alaska.

"Exxon Valdez Spill Profile." *EPA*, Environmental Protection Agency, 19 Jan. 2017, www.epa.gov/emergency-response/exxon-valdez-spill-profile.

"Ferry Turns into Lobby Boat for Congressmen." Juneau Empire News, 17 Aug. 1987.

"Hard Life on the Slope: Oil Workers Pay Price of High

Salaries." *Anchorage Daily News*, 1 July 1990, p. E1.

"Henri Says ANWR Development Has Backers." *Fairbanks Daily News Miner*, 12 Aug. 1987.

"Hodel: Crisis Help Cause of ANWR." *Daily Sitka Sentinel*, 6 Aug. 1987.

"House, Senate Leaders Differ on ANWR Timing." *Juneau Empire News*, 12 Aug. 1987.

"Key Congressmen to See ANWR." *Fairbanks Daily News Miner*, 9 Aug. 1987, p. 1.

"Letter from ARCO President." Received by Jack Smith, 29 Sept. 1987.

"Officials Don't Expect Quick Vote for ANWR." *Anchorage Daily News*, 12 Aug. 1987.

"Oil Spill Recovery Efforts Seem Futile." *Daily Sitka Sentinel*, 14 Apr. 1989, p. 12.

"An Old Environmental Warrior Faces Her Adversaries." *Anchorage Daily News*, 15 Aug. 1987.

"Panel See ANWR, Vote Maybe in '88." *Fairbanks Daily News Miner*, 11 Aug. 1987.

"Prince William Sound." *Wikipedia*, Wikimedia Foundation, 3 Feb. 2021, en.wikipedia.org/wiki/Prince_William_Sound.

"Prudhoe Bay Oil Field." *Wikipedia*, Wikimedia Foundation, 30 Mar. 2021, en.wikipedia.org/wiki/Prudhoe_Bay _Oil_Field.

"Scraps Ring Dinner Bell For Polar Bears at Prudhoe Bay." *Anchorage Daily News*, 29 Oct. 1987, p. 1.

"Senate Panel Eyes Development." *Juneau Empire News*, 11 Aug. 1987, p. 1.

"Senators: Environmentalists Lose Ground on ANWR."
    Juneau Empire Newspaper, 19 Aug. 1987.
"Statement by the Interior Secretary Don Hodel on
    Upcoming Tour of Arctic National Wildlife Refuge."
    Department of the Interior, 1987.
"Three Congressional Panels Begin ANWR Trek." *Fairbanks
    Daily News Miner*, 8 Aug. 1987, p. 1.
"Touring Senators on ANWR Trip Are Full of Superlatives
    for Alaska." *Fairbanks Daily News Miner*, 12 Aug. 1987.

Chapter 10

"The Big Letdown." *Moscow Guardian*, 18 Oct. 1991, p. 1.
"The Coup That Couldn't." *Moscow Magazine*, 1991, p. 21.
"The End: With Gorbachev's Resignation, the Soviet Union
    Dies, and an Experiment That Obsessed over the World Is
    Over." *Newsweek Magazine*, 6 Jan. 1992, p. 12.
"George H.W. Bush Address on Gorbachev Resignation." *C-
    Span.org*, www.c-span.org/video/?23549-1%2Faddress-
    gorbachev-resignation.
"Gorbachev, Last Soviet Leader, Resigns; U.S. Recognizes
    Republics' Independence." *New York Times*, 26 Dec. 1991.
"GORBACHEV RESIGNATION / COLLAPSE SOVIET
    UNION / December 25 - 1991." *YouTube*, 1 Feb. 2011,
    youtube/028gd8Sn3m0.
"Showdown in Yugoslavia: This Is Just the Beginning."
    Newsweek Magazine, 25 Mar. 1991, p. 20.
"Three Defiant Days." *Moscow Magazine*, 1991, p. 17.

Chapter 11

"1000 March Through Oroville." *Oroville Mercury Register*, 13 Dec. 1982, p. 1.

"16th Floor Leap Kills LA Woman." *Fresno Bee*, Mar. 1950.

"Bomb Attack Kill 5 in Milan and Strike 2 Churches in Rome." *New York Times*, 28 July 1993, p. 1.

"Car Bomb Kills 5 in Milan and Shake Ancient Heart of Rome." *The Independent News*, 28 July 1993.

"Demonstration March Against Racism, Ku Klux Klan." *Los Angeles Times*.

Foston, Vickie Smith. *Victoria's Secret: a Conspiracy of Silence*. Victoria Lazarian Heritage Association, 2001.

"Ratings, Reviews, and Where to Watch the Best Movies & TV Shows." *IMDb*, 7 May 2015, www.imdb.com/list/ls072516402/.

"Unidentified Woman Leaps to Death." *Modesto Bee*, 9 Mar. 1950, p. 1.

"Unidentified Woman Leaps to Death." *Sacramento Bee*, 9 Mar. 1950, p. 1.

"Woman Leaps to Death from Bank Building." *Fresno Bee*, 9 Mar. 1950, p. 1.

"Worry Is Blamed for Suicide Leap." *Fresno Bee*, 10 Mar. 1950.

Chapter 12

"Granddaughter Asks Why?" *Fresno Bee*, 3 Nov. 1997.

Chapter 13

Butte County Sheriff's Office Newsbreak, July 2012.

"Fire Forces S.F.'s Original Joe's to Close." *SFgate.com*, 12 Oct. 2007.

"Genocide Memorial Built to Honor Famed General Known as the 'George Washington of Armenia.'" *YWAM Chico News*, 14 May 2010, ywamchico.wordpress.com/2010/05/14/genocide-memorial-built-to-honor-famed-general-known-as-the-%E2%80%9Cgeorge-washington-of-armenia%E2%80%9D/.

Golin, Steve, et al. *Big Miracle*. Universal Pictures, 2012.

Groom, Winston. *Forrest Gump: a Novel*. Vintage Books, 1986.

"Haunting Family Story Revealed in 'Victoria's Secret." *Oroville Mercury Register*, 15 Sept. 2001.

Mitchell, Larry. "Memorial Marks Armenian Hero's Death at Hotel North of Chico." *The Reporter*, The Reporter, 8 Sept. 2018, www.thereporter.com/2012/08/31/memorial-marks-armenian-heros-death-at-hotel-north-of-chico/.

"Rescuers Spot Lost Family's Twig 'Help' Sign." *CNN*, Cable News Network, 20 Dec. 2007, www.cnn.com/2007/US/12/19/missing.family.found/index.html.

"Richardson Springs Sees Death of American Hero." *Oroville Daily Register*, 2 Sept. 1927, p. 1.

Writer, JULIET WILLIAMS Associated Press. "Family Found Alive Three Days after

Vanishing on Christmas Tree Hunt." *KVAL*, KVAL, 19 Dec. 2015, kval.com/news/nation-world/family-found-alive-three-days-after-vanishing-on-Christmas-tree-hunt-11-12-2015.

Zemeckis, Robert, director. *Forrest Gump*. Paramount
    Pictures, 1994.
"Obituaries." *Oroville Mercury Register*, 21 July 2012, p. 5B.

Epilogue

"A Spectacular-and Safe-Landing: Pilot Brings 727 from
    Prudhoe Bay down without Benefit of Landing Gear."
    Anchorage Daily News, 16 Oct. 1986, p. 1.

ABOUT THE AUTHOR

Vickie Smith (Foston) Odabashian began working as an educator in 1993. In 1999, she earned a Master's Degree in Sociology, and in 2001, self-published her first book, *Victoria's Secret: A Conspiracy of Silence*. Vickie and her husband, Glen, reside in Northern California near their immediate family, including five adult children and ten grandchildren (some of whom are pictured in the group photo on the next page). Learn more about her books at Vlahabooks.com.

Vickie and her husband, Glen, with some of their children, grandchildren, and grand-dogs (Photo above and on preceding page courtesy of Chris Shelton)

Made in the USA
Middletown, DE
12 February 2022

61017867R00166